Crosscurrents / MODERN CRITIQUES

Harry T. Moore, *General Editor*

H. G. WELLS
Author in Agony

Alfred Borrello

WITH A PREFACE BY

Harry T. Moore

SOUTHERN ILLINOIS UNIVERSITY PRESS
Carbondale and Edwardsville

FEFFER & SIMONS, INC.
London and Amsterdam

First published, February 1972
Second printing, August 1973
Printed in the United States of America
Designed by Andor Braun
International Standard Book Number 0–8093–0541–0
Library of Congress Catalog Card Number 77–180627

To
J. M. J.
Jude, Theresa, and my
family

Contents

Preface

In his extremely interesting Experiment in Autobiography, H. G. Wells recounts his disagreement with Henry James over the element of purpose in novels. James had once hailed the young Wells as a promising writer, but as time went on he felt that Wells was neglecting the artistic possibilities of his fiction in order to emphasize ideas. In 1915, the year before James's death, Wells cruelly parodied him in a book whose partial title is Boon. As we see in the published correspondence between James and Wells (edited by Leon Edel and Gordon Ray), James, deeply hurt, responded with admirable dignity. In the years that have passed, Wells has to a great extent faded out, while James has been lifted to a top position among all novelists.

Nevertheless, it is an extreme mistake to regard Wells as negligible. And it isn't just that his science-fiction stories can produce enjoyment in this era of moon walking. No—for Wells's total achievement is an impressive one, as Professor Borrello shows in this volume which deals expertly and attractively with all phases of this author. The early novels, somewhat Dickensian, are still fun to read, particularly Tono-Bungay (1909). But there is a great deal of good to be found in the later work, as Professor Borrello interestingly demonstrates.

At first Wells was a beaming optimist; he saw science

as a great benefit to mankind and tried to point the way
to the proper use of its techniques. Some other writers,
such as D. H. Lawrence and occasionally Bernard Shaw,
had different ideas. Lawrence consistently waged war
against the mechanization of science, and this has today
helped make him a kind of culture hero; Shaw as early as
Man and Superman could state with prophetic truth
that science would distinguish itself by primarily producing murderous weapons. It took a long time of disillusion-
ment for Wells to arrive at such conclusions and, when
he did, the effect upon him was catastrophic. Hence the
subtitle of Professor Borrello's book, Author in Agony.

I don't know of any other study of this writer which
traces his writing career so thoroughly. His experience as
an author and thinker was a great modern experience,
which this book deals with in detail. It is a thorough examination and an important summary of the work of this
man who still has so much to say to us.

HARRY T. MOORE

Southern Illinois University
November 11, 1971

Introduction

The Enlightenment, that singular glory of the eighteenth century, and the intellectual ferment which was its wake, quickly flooded Europe with the intoxicating proposition that man, were he to apply his reason properly, could turn this earth into that paradise for which he has longed from the beginning of his recorded history. Armed with this faith in human reason, men rose up to topple those institutions which mitigated against mankind's newfound belief in perfectability through its own powers rather than through any external political or supernatural force. Down came Church and State from the pedestals they had occupied. Their fall created a wave of hope which resulted in a surge of liberation that shaped the modern era and gave rise to the secular democratic state and that freedom of inquiry which resulted in Darwin's discoveries and other investigations that served only to confirm the fact that man's progress is inevitable.

But, paradoxically, the very hope man had in his future was the cause of his despair. In giving sole credit to man for any progress achieved, the Enlightenment also burdened him, by implication, with the absolute responsibility for any failure to reach the millennium. By placing an earthly paradise tantalizingly within the grasp of humanity and fixing humanity with the sole guilt for any failure to attain it, the Enlightenment prepared the ground for the defeatism and the resultant angst which plague mankind in this twentieth century. It failed to teach humanity that perfection is an ideal on which it must focus its attention and aspirations, not a state capable of total and absolute achievement. It failed to teach that to seek perfection is not necessarily to find it, nor to find it immediately. Without this essential understanding, it forced humanity into a schizophrenic position in which its youth, incapable of grasping the fundamental fact that the ideal can never be completely attained, war against the old who, through experience, have tasted the bitterness of that knowledge and have lost hope in the future.

It was in this atmosphere of hope bordering on the edge of despair, so characteristic of our own day, that H. G. Wells raised his voice at the close of the nineteenth century. At first he burned with a youthful hope for the future based upon a belief that the evil wrought by man can be reversed and eradicated through conscious and dedicated effort. That hope was fed by his own sure and steady rise from bleak poverty to relative affluence and those discoveries of science and technology which were making man's burden increasingly more comfortable to bear. Gradually, and certainly unconsciously, that hope became tinged with a note of pessimism which grew louder and clearer as he and the twentieth century grew older and more bitter. As he began to question mankind's ability to attain the millennium after his first bright and youthful hopes dimmed, his works began to reflect those themes which have come to characterize twentieth-century literature. Even the most hostile of his critics recognize that he possessed an almost uncanny ability to sense and reflect the horrors which were to become humanity's particular trials in this age.

These horrors were not so much the repulsive and unearthly monsters his fertile brain created with so much agility, nor the weapons of destruction he predicted, nor the ultimate demise he foresaw for the species. Rather, those horrors were more subtle and less comprehensible and therefore more difficult to control. Essentially they are the self-doubts which plague mankind in an era when, paradoxically, he knows more about himself and his environment than he has ever known in his entire history; they are his sense of estrangement, alienation, and loneliness, and his inability to articulate with and communicate with his fellowmen; they are his incapacity to cope with and conquer those anonymous forces which dominate his life and which are completely beyond his power to comprehend, no less overcome. And, toward the end of Wells's long life, there arose yet another, more devastating horror which he sensed in his youth but was able to suppress. That fear centered on the question of identity in a world growing ever more crowded with a sea of humanity and thereby turning ever more steadily to dehumanizing technological answers for control and order. The fear arose out of a haunting yet persistent suspicion that human reason can do little of and by itself to effect changes for the good. This suspicion threads through the characters he created in the twenties. The militant postures he gives them more often than not rest upon a doubt that they are capable of achieving anything. Ultimately, in the last years of his long life, he suspected the very existence of individuality.

Like those of Kafka, Wells's characters even in his realistic novels, despite their ability to reason in a manner far superior to their peers, are caught up in a dream-like world seeking to discover their salvation only to find that they are lost in a nightmare of man-made and reason-founded institutions and difficulties. In the angst of these characters, Wells reflects a dim recognition and report of an emerging future in which the hopes of the eighteenth century are finally and irrevocably betrayed. In that future, ironically Utopian in many aspects, a massive corrosion of will, conscience, and, ultimately, identity will be the order of the day.

The fear Wells had for the future is implied in his earlier writings in which he staunchly defends the power of the individual to overcome even the most fearsome of fates, to assert himself, and to direct and control not only his own future but the future of the entire race to that joyful heaven on earth for which it longs. The militancy of Wells's advocacy of the power of the individual, which produced a faith crediting man with the powers of a god, suggests an essential doubt of the existence of those powers.

That Wells began to lose faith in the individual and his ability to effect progress is reflected in a second phase of his work in which he pleads for action by a dedicated and superior group as a solution to mankind's problems. And, finally, approaching death, he despaired of collective action as well. And that fear which haunted even the most optimistic phases of his life asserted itself once again. Is individuality, in the light of its ineffectiveness, after all only a myth perpetrated by nature to secure the continuation of the species? In a doctoral dissertation which he submitted to London University, he pleaded that it is only an illusion. Perhaps this questioning of individuality, more than any other problem in the light of a growing population threatening to drown the species, no less the individual, is the most terrifying prophecy of a man who predicted atomic warfare and that aspect of his work which makes him most significant for our age. In any event, he deserves to be heard.

This work permits him to speak clearly and directly

by shearing away the massiveness and repetitiveness of the commentary which grew up about his work as he produced it. This commentary has the remarkable affinity for sounding the same notes. The reader will find here very little reference to Wells's socialism because it is merely the surface manifestation of something more important and deeper in his work. The reader will also discover a phase of Wells's thought too often and too conveniently overlooked by those who prefer to ride the hobbyhorse of Wellsian socialism. This is the phase in which he developed his religion of the individual which he disavowed when he no longer believed in its validity.

Of necessity, Wells's preoccupation with the fate of mankind had a direct bearing upon the art he practiced. Because ideas were preeminent with him, art was forced to take a secondary role. He rarely thought of the art he practiced. When he did, his attention was directed to those aspects of it which made his ideas more palatable to his audience. In later years, when he turned almost completely from the novel, even this attention was absent.

In this respect, Wells is eminently contemporary. In a recent survey, the *New York Times* discussed the interests of the present American college generation in art. "They," the article noted, "are more passionate about intent than about form. They want art to function . . . as a social tool." Developing this peculiarly Wellsian point of view, the article cited the findings of a psychiatrist who, when questioning the young about the purposes of art, discovered that "they say it is to mobilize, to portray degradation, to get people to take action." [1]

This point which the psychiatrist drew from his investigations is an apt description of the purposes Wells outlined for himself in his writing. As a consequence of the position Wells took, for far too long during his lifetime and after his death, critical and scholarly interest has followed his lead and has confined itself to the investigation of his ideas and their application to a world rapidly approaching the madness he predicted. Paradoxically but appropriately, however, these investigations have discovered another stratum to Wells's work. Beneath the incrustations of ideas which sound more and more naïve as we become increasingly aware of their essential impracticality, lies another, fundamentally more interesting Wells—Wells the literary figure.

Over the past ten years, the periodical, *English Literature in Transition* (through a continuing series of annotated bibliographies and articles) has served as a focal point for this interest in this country. Other manifestations of a growing awareness of Wells's work as literature are also evident and are becoming ever more numerous.[2] Worthy of separate citation, because it represents the first of a growing series of similar studies, is Gordon Ray's and Leon Edel's edition of the correspondence of Henry James and Wells (1958).[3] The volume clearly and definitively traces the development and ultimate dissolution of what must certainly be the strangest of literary friendships. More significantly, however, it establishes the broad picture of the relationships between their art and theory. At first James was drawn to Wells's novels and short stories, reveling in their freshness and their youthful vitality. Slowly, nevertheless, it became clear to James that Wells was by no means following his advice in his developing art. The inevitable and final break came when Wells satirized James in *Boon*. Ray's and Edel's volume is especially important because it served as a beginning to the important task, which is by no means complete, of placing Wells in the context of the literature of his time. All too often, his work has been studied with no such context in mind.

Also worthy of citation is Bernard Bergonzi's penetrating study of Wells's science fiction, *The Early H. G. Wells* (1961) and the work of W. Warren Wagar which began with his *H. G. Wells and the World State* (1961) and has continued in his most recent volume *H. G. Wells: Journalism and Prophecy* (1964). And certainly not to be overlooked is Richard Howard Costa's critical biography, *H. G. Wells* (1967) in the Twayne English Authors Series. Needless to say, I am indebted to these authors and to the many whom I have not cited here.

My gratitude also extends to Dr. Harry T. Moore, editor of the Crosscurrents Series, for the interest he has shown in this work and the encouragement he gave me to write this volume. My gratitude also includes Mr. Vernon Sternberg, director of the Southern Illinois University Press for his help. I must also extend my thanks to Dr. Paul Doyle, my onetime professor and now my friend, without whose help and kindness I could not have completed this work. I must also thank Mr. Thomas Hurley whose discussions with me on the subject of Wells and whose memory, which is second to none, have helped me immeasurably. I am no less grateful to Dr. Ferdinand Bachman under whose guidance as a graduate student I first developed an interest in Wells; to Dr. Jeanne Welcher Kleinfield and Dr. Edward Johnson who gave me more than moral support in those somewhat trying early days; and to Madlynne Pastor, Margery Jann, and Carol Stempion, my secretaries, who never failed to come to my aid when the mechanics of the book seemed to overwhelm me.

ALFRED BORRELLO

Brooklyn, New York
August, 1971

H. G. Wells

1

The End of the World
Youth and *The Time Machine*

Few novelists in this century, perhaps more than in any other period, can resist the delectable temptation to tailor their personal lives, thoughts, emotions into the novels they create. Many who cannot resist are relatively capable, nevertheless, of disguising their efforts to some degree. Herbert George Wells (1866–1946), however, by his own admission was capable neither of resistance nor disguise. He could not resist or disguise because he understood the events of his life in a special light. He saw mirrored in his physical and emotional anxieties and frustrations the sufferings of countless millions. He sensed

> humanity scattered over the world, dispersed, conflicting, unawakened . . . this spectacle of futility fills me with a passionate desire to end waste, to create order, to develop understanding. . . . All these people reflect and are part of the waste and discomfort of my life.[1]

As he tells us, he wanted desperately to "end the waste . . . of humanity." He believed as passionately that he was in possession of the means to fulfill his desire. Those tools he believed he had which would help him to achieve his purpose in life were his ability to write convincingly and to write copiously. At first he

1

produced a small trickle, then an even steadier stream, and finally a boiling, onrushing mass of some one hundred and fifty-six separate titles and countless shorter works.[2] Some of his books were excellent—even Henry James praised them—others were indifferent, and most were dull by contemporary standards. But all were Wells himself and not just Wells of the teens and twenties when he was lionized by critics of the world scene, political pundits, and even Stalin; but rather all were Wells of his sickly, sensitive, uncomfortable youth. They were written within the context of the distant but never fading memories of "smelly drains," grubby lodgings, and the frustrated dreams associated with his search for maturity and stability—his personal "spectacle of futility."

He was born in a shabby (the word is his own) home called Atlas House, significantly and appropriately named for one who was to believe that he had to assume the weight of the world. He never left that first home intellectually. Nothing he ever wrote, no success he was to achieve could erase the haunting memories he associated with it. He dwells on its shortcomings at length in his ponderous autobiography (1934), and shadows of it appear in the homes of some of his principal creations: Kipps (1905), George Ponderevo (1909), Polly (1910), and many other characters.

Equally haunting are the memories of his parents which cover many pages in that same autobiography. Though absolutely devoted to them, he viewed them, nevertheless, as willing victims of the society against which he battled all of his long life. He was angry at their complacency and their seeming refusal to take effective measures to improve their "place" in life. Like every new generation, he, in turn, refused to understand their lives or the secret relationships, joys and pains and heartbreaks which marked their marriage. Stirred to anger as he was by the closed minds of his parents and their distrust and fear of new and fresh ideas, he nevertheless dwells lovingly upon them as he draws their portraits page after page.

Sarah Neal Wells was the daughter of an innkeeper, literally born to serve. Apparently, Wells considered his maternal grandfather's profession ideally suited to develop the intellectually gifted and frustrated, for this is the life with which he rewards Polly's struggles. The innkeeper, however, destined his daughter for a better life. She was sent as a lady's maid to the household of Sir Henry Featherstonhaugh on whose estate, Up Park, her future husband, Joseph Wells, worked as a gardener. After their marriage, Joseph, who had never genuinely cared for the profession his father had trained him for, decided to leave the relative comfort of the estate to strike off on his own. With the financial aid offered him by a relation and a small inheritance, he opened a tiny crockery and china shop. Unfortunately his acumen as a tradesman was not equal to his ability as a cricketer for which he was locally famous.

The senior Wells was essentially a pastel figure. Wells portrays him again and again in his novels as the unsuccessful Polly ground down by the poverty assigned to him by his birth, and in the frustrations of Kipps who is unable to adjust to his wealth because of the social milieu in which he passed his youth. There are even traces of him in Albert Tewler, the antihero of *You Can't be too Careful* (1941), whose whole being is directed by caution. Though Joseph Wells was notably unsuccessful, his son cherished the belief that were he given the proper chance, he could have made for himself and his family an excellent life. That opportunity Wells affords to many of his protagonists who quickly seize it.

But reality never afforded Joseph Wells the chance to escape the drabness which he shared with most members of the lower class in Victorian England. After his marriage to Sarah, the children came with ever-increasing regularity to the young couple, and the shop which produced little revenue to begin with seemed to produce less and less each year with each addition to the growing family. Soon it became obvious to the senior Wells that no effort on his part, not even the primitive form of birth control husband and wife practiced, could stave off the inevitable failure of the shop nor secure for them a comfortable living. Fortunately, like the denouement of a Dicken's novel, help came in the form of a request from Up Park to Sarah. She took with her the young Wells, Bertie as he was called. He was ill and needed his mother's care. It was at Up Park that he was to catch the first concrete glimpse of a world for which, up to that time, he believed only vaguely that he was intended. A large part of this world was discovered when he was given freedom of the library. Sir Featherstonhaugh's collection, like those of many country aristocrats, was gathered over many generations. Rich in the works of philosophers, the books introduced the young Bertie to authors in whose lasting debt he was to remain throughout his career as a writer. There were three, however, who were to prove most influential. He read Voltaire, whose acrid satire flavors all his works and whose bitterness clouds even the most Utopian of his novels; Swift, whose hatred of the follies of the human race darts in and out of his books and whose giants reappear metamorphosed into towers of intelligence in *The Food of the Gods*; and Plato's *Republic* on which Wells was later to model his idealistic "Kingdom of God" and his "World State." [3] So fondly did he remember Up Park and what his stay there meant to him that he was to recreate it as Bladesover in *Tono-Bungay*.

But the happy life at Up Park soon came to an end almost as swiftly as it had begun, when the ever practical Sarah sensed that it was high time for Bertie to be placed, as her two older sons had been, on the road to a profitable and comfortable way of life. She sincerely believed, despite the absolute failure of her husband, that the good life was to be attained only in shopkeeping. She believed just as sincerely that in drapery was success most assured. Consequently, her youngest son was apprenticed, as were his brothers before him, to a draper. Bertie, however, was not as complacent as his brothers. He was bored and chafed at the emptiness of the life. Perhaps it was his brief taste of the better life he had been given during his stay at Up Park which forced him to walk twenty miles one day to the estate to inform his mother that he had irrevocably decided never to become a shopkeeper. His experiences behind a counter were not entirely wasted, however. He dwells on them with loathing in several of his novels.

From the moment when he made his final decision to abandon any attempt at shopkeeping until he achieved his first genuine success, the publication of *The Time Machine* (1895), his life was marked by privation. Never truly well educated—his early schooling barely gave him the rudiments of reading and writing—he chafed at his lack of knowledge. Reading widely filled some of the gaps, but only when he made the decision to move to London for a concerted attack upon his ignorance was he to take the first real step toward the life of a scientist for which he longed.

Living in London was no easier for a member of his class than life in a provincial town. In fact, it was a good deal less palatable.[4] Nevertheless, despite the thousand-and-one annoyances which marked his life, London gave him the opportunity to come into contact with minds which helped to shape the direction he was to take when he finally focused his aspirations on writing. There he seized the chance offered him to meet and eventually study biology and zoology under Thomas H. Huxley. Huxley imparted to Wells an understanding of life which kept alive the fires of pessimism which were to burn strongly even when Wells was hailed as the apostle of optimism. Huxley gave him that fear for man's future which precipitated the despair that darkened his final years.

It was Huxley's contention that Darwin's discoveries were fundamentally sound and applicable. He espoused the cause of Darwinism when to do so was to call down upon one's head a whirlwind of abuse. He had, ultimately, to defend his beliefs against the attacks of Gladstone, the prime minister. Though he fought long and bitter battles in defense of the theories he held, Huxley never claimed that evolution would result in the millenium for mankind as some had. Rather, he foresaw defeat and ultimate annihilation in mankind's future. He held that the species, by the very evolutionary process many hailed as progress and civilization, had developed to the point where it was engaged in a massive battle with its society, the world, and those cosmic forces loose in the universe which cannot be defeated and which will finally destroy it. But far more devastating than those unknown and uncontrollable cosmic forces is man's most powerful enemy—himself. Huxley contended that man is at war with man and, more tragically, he is at war with himself.

But there was yet another equally powerful force at work within Wells. That force was the element he found most irritating in his mother—her faith. She was literally possessed by what he calls a "Low Church Theology" which had at its core a stern, angry God the Father, the source of whose actions could invariably be discovered in a burning, almost jealous resentment of his creatures. This anger was caused by the sin he was able to identify in even the most holy of his ungrateful creatures. This sin was generally vaguely sexual even when not directly connected with the tentative explorations of a growing boy or the more pronounced and obvious actions of adults. For Sarah, this theology was adequate and satisfying, though she could not consciously trace to such transgressions the source of the poverty and pain doled out in heaping measures to herself and her family. Hers was a negative faith—a faith built on prohibition, proscription, hedged with fears not bound in any way with love, the love Wells felt so great a need for even as a child, the love for which he searched in so many of the sordid affairs he was to engage in as success crowned his efforts as a writer.

At first, Bertie was eager to follow his mother's lead in religion, but early in his life he began to suspect the existence of this cantankerous deity, perhaps because he saw that this god was obviously turning a deaf ear to his and his mother's prayers. But more likely, he began to realize, with the rationalization of youth, that angry as this god was, he made no move to punish him for the minor sexual adventures which were occupying his mind and body more and more. Then, Wells tells us, he had a dream.

> I had a dream of Hell so preposterous that it blasted that resort [as a basis for belief] out of my mind forever . . . there was Our Father in a particularly malignant phase . . . I saw no devil in my vision; my mind in its simplicity went straight to the responsible fountainhead. The dream pursued me into the daytime. Never had I hated God so intensely. And then suddenly the light broke through to me and I knew that God was a lie.[5]

Suspect as this "revelation" may be, his recording of it is significant because it represents one of the major preoccupations of his entire career as a writer. He was to pursue all through his long life some fit substitute for the God who "was a lie." He rejected belief in a deity who possessed those qualities which he subconsciously admitted were necessary to end the "spectacle of futility" which was his understanding of the plight of humanity. Sarah's god was all-powerful, cranky though he may be. He held out to his creatures, though he seemingly despised them, the promise of a perfect life which Huxley believed was impossible to achieve. But it was this very level of human perfection for which Wells hungered. He saw perfection as the only answer to the poverty and pain suffered by him and those countless millions whom he believed he represented. In rejecting Sarah's god, he was forced to reject the Heaven he offered. But Wells could not reject the longing for that Heaven which consumed him and directed everything he wrote and every speech he gave. He had only one route which he could take to satisfy that longing. There must exist somewhere in someone or something a force more powerful than his mother's invisible and omnipotent deity which would crown with success his search for human perfection. That search came to focus in his first novel, *The Time Machine* (1895).

But more suffering was to be Well's lot before the publication of that work. After studying under Huxley, he turned to teaching to sustain himself though he always thought of himself as a man of science. Teaching did not prove to be as lucrative as he had hoped. Much of the anguish which was his in this period of his life is reflected in *Love and Mr. Lewisham* (1900). While teaching, he suffered an injury to his kidney which was followed by a siege of tuberculosis. He was forced to return home to convalesce. During this period of inaction, for want of anything better to do, he turned to writing. He produced two scientific textbooks, some short stories and, finally, after much revision, *The*

Time Machine. Its unexpected success forced him to turn to writing for his living.

Its appeal was immediate. Though some recognized elements of Jules Verne's method in it, it projected a vitality and youthful hope that Verne never displayed. Its public, though sensing something new in the tale, failed to grasp what Wells was trying to do. Its significance in terms of his life's work, as a consequence, remained clouded for generations. Contributing factors to this lack of clarity were the scientific patina Wells gave it with all the sociological implications arising from it. Despite the problems it presented, it is, even in this day, a stimulating story.

The Time Traveller's device carries him into the future. In his travels he witnesses the rise and fall of civilizations and their rise again to more brilliant heights. The Time Machine comes to rest in A.D. 802,701, a period when the most exalted of these civilizations is in decline. It is a Huxleyan world. He encounters the humans of the period and discovers the species divided into two groups: the devourers (the Morlocks) and the devoured (the Eloi). The latter are four feet high, seemingly sexless, beautiful, graceful but indescribably frail creatures who have forgotten all art and industry. The Morlocks, monstrous apelike creatures, live in subterranean caves. They are the mechanics of this age who keep the Eloi, but come up out of their holes to feed on them in the moonless nights.

At this point, the Time Traveller clearly assumes the part of Wells commenting upon the society of his time. The Morlocks in their avariciousness suggest the role assigned by Wells to the capitalists in his young mind; and the poor, sexless, supine Eloi—who freely permit themselves to be cannibalized by the Morlocks—suggest the much oppressed class into which he, Wells, was born. What we are presented here, in a sense, is not so much a picture of the future, but rather a representation of the present—the turn of the century.

In this two-class society of Eloi and Morlocks, love plays no part. It is only with the appearance of the Time Traveller upon the scene that love, and the power that Wells believes it possesses, furtively rears its gentle albeit sexless head. Weena, an Eloi woman, becomes attracted to him, first from gratitude—he rescues her from drowning—and then out of affection. Unknown to him, before his departure to his own time, she places a flower in his pocket, a fragile token of her affection. It is what this flower represents, when he discovers it in his pocket, which proves to be the impetus for his desire to journey once again into the future to discover the key which will prevent the extinction of mankind whose last, dying gasp he has so vividly witnessed.

Though there is reference here to a need for some form of salvation, there is no mention of a god who can save his creatures, nor a religious creed postulated as a guide for that salvation. Rather, there is a suggestion that mankind must be saved through the efforts of man himself, through an individual who, though thoroughly human, is motivated by an unselfish love of humanity and who is willing to confront the dangers, horrors, and agony of the unknown in an attempt to effect that salvation. That figure, in the guise of the Time Traveller and the other protagonists he was to create, Wells believed was himself.[6]

Here then in his first novel is the direction, in microcosm, which Wells's creative life was to take. Like the Time Traveller, Wells has his "time machine" which will help him in his ceaseless, never varying search for the answer to mankind's ultimate problem. Unlike the Time Traveller, however, Wells's machine is not made of ivory and chrome but of pen and ink and paper.

When approached from another point of view, *The*

Time Machine also suggests the several paradoxes which were constantly to haunt Wells in his search for the salvation of his species in his writing. The attempted solution of these paradoxes was to affect the direction his writing took as well as occupy his attention for the remainder of his life as a writer and was to end in frustration. The first rests squarely upon his firm belief in Huxley's hypothesis that the species is doomed to extinction. He depicts the Time Traveller standing at the edge of an ocean witnessing the death of the world whose only inhabitants are "monstrous crab-like creatures." Yet the scene, depressing as it is, does not drive from his heart the belief that he could save his race. Like his character, Wells clung unflaggingly to the hope throughout most of his life that some concerted action on the part of the individual, notably men like himself, could frustrate mankind's inevitable disappearance from the globe. This hope animates most of his protagonists even when they are confronted, like the Time Traveller, with seemingly impossible situations. With this firm belief in mind, Wells campaigned through his books (*The Idea of a League of Nations,* 1918; *The Way to a League of Nations,* 1918; *The Salvaging of Civilization,* 1921; etc.) and in personal appearances throughout the world for the unity of mankind which would direct the species to its true purpose— its own salvation. Only toward the end of his life, which witnessed the two world wars he had foreseen and the reality of the atom bomb and other horrible weapons his active imagination had invented, was that hope finally killed.

Further, the novel presents us with the paradox of individuality which figures as an important theme in Well's work as throughout the twentieth-century novel. The Morlocks and Eloi are indistinguishable within their own groups. Even their sex lies hidden. All Eloi have long, flowing hair so reminiscent of the youth of our day. Even their very clothing mitigates against individuality. Only the Time Traveller and Weena, for a brief moment, achieve identity. They achieve it because they actively identify themselves with a purpose other than that of the group. But identification of such a nature means involvement. And involvement brings with it danger and pain. The Time Traveller learns this principle only too well as do all of Wells's protagonists. When the Time Traveller proceeds to rescue Weena from drowning, he acts alone without the help of the Eloi who stand about dumbly disinterested in the fate of one of their kind. Weena, in turn, achieves her individuality when she identifies herself with her rescuer and offers him her love such as it is. Her pain comes when he leaves her.

The question must be asked at this point, as Wells most certainly must have asked himself time and time again, why the struggle? Why endure the pain of identification, the heartache of individuality when no struggle, no pain, no heartache can ultimately, as Huxley believed alter the destiny of mankind? After all, though the Time Traveller believes that he can frustrate that destiny, what his eyes see denies that belief.

Wells's reason for the struggle, for the endurance of the pain and the heartache begins with a rejection. This rejection is the chief motivating force of his characters and is the quality which sets them apart from their peers. Essentially, Wells rejects Christianity and its understanding of mankind as he rejected his mother's faith. He rejects it as insufficient motivation for the struggle. To suffer here on earth in a never-ending battle for a vague promise of an even vaguer joy in Heaven, he labels as insanity. Moreover, to believe that this earthly existence is a transitory phase of a greater, more enduring life is to him a child's dream. The only reality for

Wells and for his characters is the "now" of life on this earth. Moreover, he rejects the passivity Christianity preaches. While he does not deny that pain and suffering are part of man's lot, he insists that struggle is also part. Merely to suffer and to "turn the other cheek" is to consign oneself to defeat.[7]

Because Wells believed that only an earthly reality exists, he affirmed that one must probe this earthly life for the reasons why the futile struggle against man's destiny must be waged. In that examination he discovered the source of man's doom, as Huxley did, in man himself. The species, he believed, is cursed with a fundamental yearning for the *status quo*, for a changeless existence in which life proceeds at the same pointless pace as it has always proceeded—witness its desire for a never-ending Heaven. His mother's willing acceptance of her "place" in life was an example of this desire. The Morlocks and the Eloi are additional examples of this yearning. The Eloi never dream of opposing the Morlocks. They are content, like the lower class of Wells's own day, to live out their dreamlike and more than childish lives until required for some Morlock's dinner. Not even the horror of witnessing one of their companions being dragged bodily into their enemies' lair disturbs their composure. They want nothing but the softness of their lives uncomplicated by thoughts of the future. Wells must have seen their equivalents in many a pub and on many a street in London. But the Eloi are not alone in their desire to keep things as they are. The Morlocks, the capitalists of the future, also want nothing to change. Why should they pursue another course when there are sufficient Eloi to satisfy even the most insatiable appetite? Moreover, the Eloi are easy to keep, and the search for a new source of food would divert their attention from the machines to which they are dedicated.

Yet, cursed as mankind is with this yearning for the *status quo* which will be part of it until its end, the species is also blessed in each of its generations with the happy few whose desire for change is so burning, so all consuming that this small band can move the mass to a higher rung on the ladder of progress. The Time Traveller is such a one. Though he identifies with the Eloi, he cannot rest content with their fate. The pages of human history (and indeed Wells's books) are replete, Wells instructs us in his *Outline of History*, with examples of men imbued with the same desires.

All of Wells's novels are based on this twofold concept of humanity. He literally divides his characters into two camps: the minor figures who, like the Morlocks and Eloi, represent the inertia of the masses; and the central figure—the happy individual who, like the Time Traveller and himself, despite the pain of such positive action, determines to alter his social, emotional, economic, or intellectual position. Polly is a member of this group. And the list could go on and on: The Angel (*The Wonderful Visit*, 1895); Dr. Moreau (*The Island of Dr. Moreau*, 1896); Griffin (*The Invisible Man*, 1897); Lewisham (*Love and Mr. Lewisham*, 1900); Ann Veronica (*Ann Veronica*, 1909); Stratton (*The Passionate Friends*, 1913).

In *The War of the Worlds* (1898), the only character who filters through the horrors wrought by the creatures from Mars is the unnamed individual who devises a plan for the continued existence of his species, and by willingly identifying himself with mankind, like the Time Traveller, he accepts the pain and danger-filled future. Paradoxically, he also receives an individuality in the act. Others, however, crumble in the face of impending doom. A clergyman, in a bitter monologue, sums up Christianity's failure to cope with the disaster. Echoing his frustration are the big guns booming away in the distance in an equally futile attempt to destroy the monsters. They are as efficacious as the cockchafers droning in the nearby hedgerow.

A recognition, then, of these two vital yet contradictory forces in the human species; the dynamic and the passive, serves as the basis for the development of Well's characters. Further, they serve as the foundation of his philosophy of struggle which motivates these characters. That philosophy Wells calls his "religion." [8] It is an ironic appellation because he rejected, on the one hand, a faith with an infinite God, a hierarchy, a Heaven and a Hell, only to establish another "faith" with similar attributes. For his faith has a "god." All who are "dissatisfied" with things as they are, all who sense the need for change, all who identify themselves with others and thereby become intimately involved with the struggle that follows, all in short who, like the Time Traveller, the unidentified character in *The War of the Worlds*, and all of the protagonists in Wells's novels "experience" an "idea" of this "god." This deity, however, has none of the marks of the Christian God about him. He is not infinite, omnipresent, nor all-powerful. He does not suffer passively on a cross. Indeed, were Wells's god to be pictured on a cross, he would be portrayed as having ripped one hand from the nail which held it and clenching it in defiance and anger at his tormentors. Wells's god more closely resembles the dynamic aspects of humanity. He is constantly engaged in a painful struggle for identity during the course of which he grows in strength, power, and boldness. Further, he knows that ultimately his efforts must be directed to the salvation of mankind from inevitable extinction.[9]

But who is this "god"? The answer, Wells tells us, lies in identifying the principles which govern his operation—remember, he is a finite god. Wells maintains that he exists in the minds of men but only when those minds, like those of his protagonists, are moved to act by a desire for change evidenced by that sense of "dissatisfaction" Wells maintained is so essential. He operates, therefore, through men, not, however, as a separate entity as does the Christian God. Mankind is not his puppet. Each man who acts to change his way of life in any fashion is god.

What Wells is telling us in his novels and in the philosophy which guides them is that man's supreme accomplishment, the salvation of his species from annihilation, can be effected not through an old, half-understood, outmoded theology with its vision and aspirations locked on another world; but rather salvation can only be effected through a realistic theology based upon man's own strengths and upon successful examples of what mankind could do were it to martial those strengths and direct them properly. One of these successful examples Wells believed was himself. As he believed that the pain of his early life reflected the anguish of millions, he more firmly believed that the life he had achieved through struggle could be achieved, as he proves in his novels, by anyone who understands that the small voice of dissatisfaction gnawing away at complacency is the voice of god—man the combatant—fighting for his life.

2

The Search for Salvation Begins

In shifting the burden of perfecting humanity from the shoulders of a cantankerous deity who offers that perfection as a reward for the suppression of natural desires and delivering it into the hand of each member of the species, Wells created obvious difficulties for mankind. These difficulties he reflects in the tangled lives of the protagonists in his novels. He now had a crop of potential saviors who, though driven by their love for their fellow creatures and a burning desire to change the direction of their lives and to accept the pain and danger that change implies, are, after all, only human despite their ultimate desire to forestall the extinction of the race. Wells was aware that man's zeal often cools in the face of distractions. He knew that man's single-mindedness often splinters in the face of delay and opposition. He knew that man, even the most superior of men,—like the Time Traveller, Clissold (*The World of William Clissold*), and Benham (*The Research Magnificent*)—requires a force to prevent his straying from his purpose. He knew that force must be as rigid and as compelling as the hellfire and damnation the propagandists of his mother's god used to force his rebellious creatures into submitting to his will. Ironically, Wells discovered the nucleus of that force which would keep his "god-men," his believers, in the paths of righteousness in those weapons Christianity used so effectively. These two all-powerful weapons, "salvation" and "damnation," he sensed could be readily applied to his new and more vital "faith." These concepts he builds into the very marrow of his characters who, while often not overtly aware of either state, act only as they are attracted to the one and repelled by the implications of the other. Unlike Christianity, however, Wells believed in no middle ground, no purgatory in which those of lesser dedication might be purified and made fit for salvation. No, Wells firmly believed that everyone must ultimately choose the one or the other state. Once the choice is made, it is irrevocable. And thus it is in his novels.

Again, unlike Christianity's, Wells's salvation is not concerned with and does not offer a heaven of eternal bliss after death. Rather, his understanding of salvation is limited to the present existence and is marked by a constant and never-ending struggle waged not against the world, the flesh, and the devil; but against ignorance, convention, complacency, and conservatism. Periods of relative calm might touch the lives of the saved, but these can be but momentary lulls in the battle which can only end with death. Struggle which never ceases, privation, emotional, spiritual, and even physical pain are necessary ingredients because salvation demands that the individual refuse to accept the limitations imposed upon him by the social position he has inherited with birth, a poor education, his nationality, his poverty, or any factor or combination of factors which impede the development of his potentialities to the maximum in his search for his unique identity.

As an object lesson for the faithful and in an attempt to elaborate the implications of his beliefs, Wells produced a novel, *The Undying Fire* (1919). It is essentially a retelling of the biblical tale of Job and the suffer-

ings sent him by God to test his faith. The story, however, is related in Wellsian terms. Job Huss is the headmaster of Woldingstanton Public School which is the
successful product of years of struggle on his part to
break the pattern of the conventional and narrow education offered in the English public schools. A true believer, he has based the curriculum on the teaching of
history in terms of the Wellsian tenets of human solidar-
ity and faith in God the Invisible King. This he has accomplished despite the constant opposition from those
of lesser vision. Suddenly, after a number of years of
relative calm, he sees all that he has built through sacrifice and struggle dissolve before his very eyes. His enemies have him dismissed as headmaster; his teachings
are reversed; his confidants desert him. He cannot realize
that he has become the object of a wager between the
Wellsian god and the forces of evil against which he
fights for his very existence. Job is to be tested and sorely
tried, as was his biblical namesake, to prove the validity
of the faith he holds.

Not only does Job lose all that he has gained through
diligence and hard work, but he is smitten by an illness
which is diagnosed as an advanced state of cancer.
Wracked by terrible pain and lying on his sickbed shortly
before he is to be operated on, he is visited by three
friends whose comforting words add immeasurably to
his agony. Tortured and depressed, Job nevertheless
holds fast to his faith as they discuss the affairs of the
world now in the midst of the war. He is tempted during the course of the discussion almost to the point of
surrendering his beliefs. He begins to realize, however,
what he represents. He knows that he is Job Huss, alone
in a hostile world, aware of the path he must take to
attain his personal salvation and the salvation of those
in his charge. The comforters would have him relinquish
his hard-won identity to retire to a way of life which

caused him agonies to escape. He also senses, however, that he is more than the suffering Job Huss. He is also mankind wracked by the cancer of the war which is raging, the war which was directly caused by attitudes expressed by his comforters. He arrives at the conclusion that these same attitudes, unless expunged, will, after the cessation of hostilities, once again begin the crucifixion of humanity unless they are resisted with determination and courage. These comforters are embodiments of all that is loathesome in England: its conservatism, its unwillingness to profit by past mistakes, its pettiness, its devotion to the ephemeral, its love of comfort. Finally, in a moment of heroism, Job rejects them and their blandishments to face the operation bravely, firmly convinced that should he not survive, he will die believing in those principles which have guided his life. The operation is a success. Huss recovers completely. The book ends with his determination to rebuild what he has lost.

As Wellsian salvation is the converse of that of the Christian, so too is his concept of damnation different. Wellsian damnation does not consist of an eternity of pain. On the contrary, it is a comfortable state, for it produces an animallike, peace-filled indifference because it permits the individual to avoid the necessity of identification. It gives the individual license to accept the coloration of the mass, to yield to the corrosiveness of creature comforts, to relax in the arms of outworn social and moral conventions.[1] More specifically, the damned become less aware of their fellowmen, less interested in them as individuals, and more alive to devious ways in which others can be used and if need be, discarded. There are many damned in the pages of Wells's novels. The Eloi and Morlocks are of that state and so is Sumner (*The Dream*, 1924) who seduces the unsuspecting Hetty after falsely pledging his love to her. Bechamel

(*The Wheels of Chance*, 1896), though less obviously, is also damned. His speciality is playing upon the weaknesses of others to attain his end. He is a married author who plots to take advantage of Jessie Milton, an imaginative and romantic girl. And too often, the damned in Wells's novels are pillars of society like the Buntings (*The Sea Lady*, 1902), Lord Justin (*The Passionate Friends*, 1913), Lady Syndenham (*Joan and Peter*, 1917), and countless others, all of whom work mightily to preserve the position which they have inherited or to which they aspire. In all of this speculation, on salvation and damnation conducted at first within the dimension of his novels and later in his nonfiction, Wells sensed something of the plight of modern man as he acts in a world designed by the machine for a life of material comfort never dreamed of before by his species. While Wells was quick to understand that man must travel through the fires of social unrest if all levels of society are to enjoy this comfort, he sensed, as Huxley did, that the real devil is man himself. How delightfully easy it is to be "damned." How pleasant it is to lose oneself in comfort, to forget the countless irritants which abound in a life where struggle is still necessary. His *Time Machine* reflects that ease, as do so many of his novels including his last, *You Can't Be Too Careful*.

Lewisham (*Love and Mr. Lewisham*, 1900) discovers, early in his career, the difficulty of resisting the status of the damned. When the novel opens, the reader finds the eighteen-year-old Lewisham, an assistant master in a suburban school, planning a wonderful schema, an outline for his attack on the world which is designed to carry him to the highest situation in science and politics. The plan is founded on hard work and efficiency. Though imbued with a youthful, burning desire to change the direction of his life, he has not counted on the wiles of his nature and those restrictions society has placed on satisfying his natural appetites. He finds himself too weak-willed to resist the first temptation to deviate from his schema. That first temptation comes in the form of the attractive, but common, Ethel Henderson whom he meets on a visit to friends. Though entirely innocent, their meetings result in a scandal which causes Lewisham to lose his position.

Undaunted, he returns to his original plan and enrolls as a guinea-a-week student at the Normal School of Science, South Kennsington. For a time, he appears to be moving ahead according to plan. Miss Heydinger, a fellow student, falls in love with him. Intellectually superior to Ethel, she senses Lewisham's potential and is willing to help him to achieve his goals. Unfortunately, Ethel comes back into his life. There are armies of Ethels in Wells's novel. They represent all those negative elements of his class against which he fought for his own personal success. When young, they are all attractive, but soon lose whatever prettiness they had in the harshness of the lives they lead. They are incapable of ever bettering themselves because they can conceive of no better life. Unknown to themselves, they destroy the Lewishams because they cannot understand their aspirations. Yet they are paradoxically, guiltless because they are unaware of what they do.

Ethel and Lewisham meet at a séance given to the students by Lagune, a rich but very credulous amateur spiritualist. The "medium" is her stepfather who, during the course of the session, is uncovered as a fraud. To save her from his influence and to satisfy his own yearning for her, Lewisham marries her. The marriage signals the end of his career. He fails at his examinations; the problems of earning a living plague him. Soon the glamour of his marriage and the fulfillment he desired fades. The couple quarrel; they become reconciled by the prospect of the coming of a child. Lewisham soon ceases to struggle. He learns that it is far simpler to scrap his schema and accept the life that seems to open itself to him. He will be a schoolmaster for the remainder of his life.

Edward Ponderevo (*Tono-Bungay*, 1908) is very much like Lewisham in his discovery that damnation is not as horrible as it first appears. The success of his patent medicine and the life of luxury that success brings make it a relatively simple matter to forget the morality of the situation and his duty to those who seek his nostrum as a cure for their ailments. For Wells, Ponderevo symbolizes a popular species of mentality— those who have not awakened to the greater issues of life. George, his nephew, is at first attracted to his uncle's philosophy which has at its core the belief that the world is an uncharted jungle open for exploration and exploitation only to "adventurers" willing to risk all for success. In this philosophy Wells saw waste. The aimless fever of trade and moneymaking and pleas- ure-seeking mitigates against those values he believed should be the motivation in human activity. But the greatest waste he saw lay in the waste of humanity.

George Ponderevo, like the young Wells he and Lewi- sham resemble, grew up in the shadow of Bladesover House, where his mother was housekeeper. Again like the young Wells, George soon became aware of the sharp distinctions which the English mentality imposes upon its society. The neighborhood about the manor house is a miniature England supporting each of the social classes, from gentry to laborers, in much the same manner as the remainder of the country.

George is away much of the time at school. During one of his vacations at Bladesover, he learns for the first time of the class to which he belongs. He falls in love with the Honorable Beatrice Normandy and, when he battles with her half-brother, Archie Garvel, she sup-

ports Archie rather than George in the quarrel. The
lesson she teaches him of class distinctions and the
loyalties they breed results in an untenable emotional
position. As a consequence, his mother feels it best to re-
move him from Bladesover. She sends him to live with
her brother, whose family is even more narrowly religious than she. There his life becomes more unbearable. Finally, she delivers him into the hands of his
father's brother, Edward Ponderevo, a none too successful chemist to whom he is apprenticed.

Like many Wellsian characters in whom the potentialities for salvation lurk, Edward is a restless, moody,
dissatisfied yet unconsciously funny individual. Like
Lewisham, he does not recognize the true source of this
dissatisfaction—a desire for salvation, the voice of god
fighting for life. He conceives of this dissatisfaction
only as a desire to expand his horizons, to live the good
life of the upper classes, in short, to make a good deal of
money as quickly as possible. Foolish investments, however, lead to financial ruin. He loses his shop and the
small sum entrusted to him by his sister-in-law for
George's future. Edward and his gentle, patient, and loving wife, Susan, are forced to leave the town in disgrace.

George, however, remains. His life at this point paral-
lels his creator's to a large degree. His spirits are crushed
by the privations and drudgery which mark his life.
Finally, he determines to compensate for the hours of
emptiness which mark the movement of his days by
matriculating at the University of London for his
bachelor of science degree. In London, during one of
his walks—his inexpensive entertainment—he meets by
chance his uncle who cryptically whispers the name
"Tono-Bungay" to him. George is rather bewildered by
the reference but puts it out of his mind as he becomes
increasingly absorbed in his studies. He pursues them
diligently until he meets Marion Ramboat, the girl who

is to become his wife. Like Lewisham's Ethel, Marion is not George's intellectual equal. As colorless as Ethel, she nevertheless represents an object of desire to George. He wants desperately to marry her but realizes his studies will never give him the money he needs. One day, on one of his long rambles through London, he sees a billboard advertising "Tono-Bungay." He remembers the strange conversation he had with his uncle. He writes to him. In return, he receives a telegram offering him employment at three hundred pounds a year. After a week of indecision during which he is pulled between his ideals and the joys, particularly sexual fulfillment, which money can bring, George gives in and decides to cast his lot with his uncle.

Tono-Bungay is a patent medicine, essentially a stimulant, most inexpensive to produce and only slightly injurious to health. Through it, and the new and bold methods of advertising which catapult it into a national product, Wells suggests the fundamental evil which corrupts society. In one of the first of the "Madison Avenue" novels, Wells reveals the power of advertising. The utterly useless Tono-Bungay becomes the poor man's damnation. Through its stimulating effects, the poor, the sick, the emotionally disturbed can achieve that peace for which they yearn. But the peace is ironic and false because the medicine does not cure, but merely cloaks the symptoms of malaise and disease. With the symptoms hidden, these debilitating and destructive viruses of mind and body can continue even more effectively to obliterate the user's humanity by stilling the voice of unrest which is Wells's god calling for life.

But the effects of Tono-Bungay are even more devastating to its manufacturers. George and Marion finally marry now that George has become more financially stable. But the marriage is not a happy one. George,

like Lewisham before him, cannot quite understand the
dimensions of his sexual appetite, which he believes
can be sated within the convention of marriage. This
is a common failing in Wells's protagonists. George is
incapable of seeing that Marion can never satisfy him
completely. She in turn, like Ethel, educated in the narrow conventions of her class, clings to marriage as the
means to that security, emotional as well as financial,
for which she yearns. Ultimately, despite her misgivings,
she divorces George when she discovers his affair with
Effie Rink, one of the secretaries in his office. After the
divorce, George plunges back into his studies, which he
had abandoned for his uncle's business.

Edward Ponderevo, meanwhile, has become fabu-
lously wealthy, yet somehow, the restlessness and dissatisfaction which plagued him in his poverty still remain. He dashes into newer and more daring financial
enterprises, all launched with funds realized from the
growing sales of Tono-Bungay. The nostrum has, by
this time, become the national narcotic. He creates a
huge corporation ironically called Domestic Utilities,
shortened to Do-Ut, which gives him newer dimensions
of wealth and prestige. The wealth is reflected in the
ever more grandiose houses he acquires with every rung
he advances up the ladder of success. Finally, his aspirations focus, significantly, on an accomplishment of
splendor, a huge palace atop Crest Hill on which three
hundred workmen are constantly laboring.

In the face of his uncle's activity, George becomes
more and more ill at ease with the life supplied him by
his share of the Tono-Bungay swindle. As an antidote
to his growing discontent, he throws himself with
greater desperation into his research and his inventions.
He begins experimenting with gliders and balloons.
After an accident caused by an abortive experiment, he
meets Beatrice again. She nurses him back to health,

and the two fall in love. She refuses to marry him, however, despite his vast wealth and her love for him. He begins to realize that his money, his scientific interests and accomplishments, and his physical attraction do not erase the fact of his birth into a class significantly lower than Beatrice's. He is still the servant, she the mistress.

Suddenly, almost as suddenly as it has become a success, the top-heavy speculation of Edward Ponderevo collapses. Once again on the verge of bankruptcy and disgrace, Edward clutches at any means of saving himself from financial ruin and the loss of his great, still uncompleted house which has become the motivating force in his life. That house has come to symbolize, in its incomplete state, the life he has led—an enormous number of richly decorated rooms, most of which lead nowhere, their basic pattern altered by whim and the total equalling nothing and incapable of completion. In a larger sense, that house suggests all that man has accomplished in every century of his existence and foreshadows his final end if his efforts are not properly directed to the salvation of his species.

George does his best to help his uncle. He plans a voyage to Mordet Island to capture by trickery a huge cargo of quap, an ore containing canadium, one of the ingredients necessary for the production of a new and more improved lamp filament. The filament could save the Ponderevo empire. Ironically, that salvation which hangs, so to speak, by a filament, never occurs. The expedition is abortive as is every other measure applied to stave off financial ruin.

Knowing his uncle faces arrest, George transports him to France in his airship. The escape is a success, but Edward becomes dangerously ill and dies before his wife can reach him. Thoroughly depressed, George returns to England and throws himself into a twelve-day love affair with Beatrice, who still refuses to marry him but has no prejudices against the clandestine affair. George is repelled by the position she takes and begins to lose all hope for a society which spawned such attitudes. He becomes a caustic critic of the degeneration in England of which such antiquated social postures are a symptom and turns his attention to designing destroyers which, he hopes, will hasten the day of change.

In all of Wells's hatred for the social system which raised up the Beatrices and forced the Lewishams and the Edward Ponderevos to hunger after those material joys which still the voice of god within the individual, he was not hard on the members of his own class who succumb to the pleasures of damnation. He does not condemn Lewisham's capitulation or turn Edward Ponderevo into a caricature of the voracious capitalist, because he recognized that to "give in," to "relax" in the arms of the comfort they sought is simple and all too often irresistible to the poor who have been denied material joys. The surrender is easy even if the cost, one's own identity and purpose as a human being, is outrageously high. Wells's fears in this regard suggest the fears of many of our own younger generation who, born into many of the comforts he dreaded so much yet found so basically appealing to human nature, reject them to seek something akin to the salvation for which he yearned.

Wells believed, as perhaps our "flower people," do that despite the superficial unattractiveness of salvation, every thinking individual must struggle to attain it, for in that state lies the only response, the only gesture mankind is capable of making to the vision of the inevitable death of its species witnessed by the Time Traveller. Can then the salvation of everyone effectively stave off the destruction of mankind? Wells's answer is no. What it can do, however, is contribute to the only "good" possible in a world such as ours.[2]

Wells understood, however, the weakness of man and

most especially the weakness of members of his own class from whom the comforts of the good life had been withheld for so long. Moreover, he understood the difficulty of moving the species to act to achieve the good through philosophical argumentation which promises, after all, so painful a reward for the immense effort expended. He proposed, therefore, a plan or code of conduct which was to guide his god-men to their final salvation. This is the code which directs the actions of his protagonists. It is based upon a single principle which guided his life. He thought so much of it that he cites it in his autobiography as well as in *The History of Mr. Polly.*

> If you want something sufficiently take it and damn the consequences . . . if life is no good for you change it. Never endure a way of life that is dull and dreary because after all the worst thing that can happen to you, if you fight and go on fighting to get out, is defeat, and that is never certain to the end which is death.[3]

How attractive this principle must have sounded to the youth of his day and to members of the lower class who, when Wells proposed it, were beginning to sense the power which was theirs through the education once denied them and through the wealth coming to them from their increasing participation in the growing industrialization. Might not Wells be correct? Might he not hold the key to success? the answer? The enormous sales of his books which reflected the success of his formula suggest that the code had struck a responsive nerve, for this is the principle which guided the young Wells who refused to remain a draper's assistant and a member of the class into which he was born. This is the principle which guides the Time Traveller who, against all sane advice, mounts the Time Machine to search for a better life. It is the principle which guides the first steps of Lewisham and directs the successes of his fellow characters like Polly.

Polly (*The History of Mr. Polly*, 1910)is an individual spiritually akin to Lewisham, Edward Ponderevo, and his nephew George. Like the three, he is restless, dissatisfied, longing for a fulfillment of his potentialities he knows his social status is incapable of providing. And, more significantly, like these and all of Wells's creations who display any signs of the presence of his god within them, he is intellectually young and filled with a lust for life which sets him at odds with his peers.

At first, despite Polly's longing to conquer new worlds and scale the heights of great achievement, he forces himself to accept the way of life open to him by his social position. The son of a small shopkeeper, Alfred Polly seems doomed to follow in the footsteps of his father. He leaves school at the age of fourteen barely equipped with the rudiments of learning and is apprenticed, much like his creator, in a drapery shop. After losing his place, he tries various other "cribs" until the death of his father provides him with a small legacy. He is persuaded by his cousins to invest it in a haberdasher's shop in Fishbourne. His fortune seems assured. There is only one element lacking; this is soon supplied by marriage to Miriam Larkins, his cousin. But soon, like Lewisham, he discovers his dreams turning sour. The shop does not prosper nor does his marriage. Much to his chagrin, he does not find fulfillment in Miriam as he had hoped he would.

When the reader first meets Polly, he is suffering from a severe case of indigestion which is the result of the frustrations he encounters in the life circumstance forces him to lead. While there is humor in the picture of Polly sitting on the stile clutching his aching stomach, there is also pathos. He is an appealing figure because beneath the pain, the inadequacies of his marriage, his daily life, there still burns that hot, hard flame of rebellion. Here is the Time Traveller, Lewisham, George Ponderevo, and Wells in yet another disguise. Polly guards that flame of rebellion in his heart of hearts and will not permit it to die. The thought of escape from his narrow life into a life of fulfillment and freedom gives him the strength to go on. He waits, but the opportunity to escape never presents itself. Finally, in utter desperation, he dwells on the thought of suicide and makes plans to end his life. Then he thinks of his wife. Though she is one of the causes of his angst, he cannot leave her a widow unprotected.

He plans his death to take place in a fire he will start in his shop, and takes care to contrive the situation to appear as an accident in order that the insurance on his life and his business will be paid. He meditates on his life of misery before he begins to dispatch himself with the razor he has sharpened for that purpose. His soul is cramped by the memory of lost opportunity. Why had he not seized the things he thought beautiful and pursued the things he had desired? Why had he not "fought for them, taken any risk for them, died rather than abandon them? They were the things that mattered. . . . He had been a fool, a coward and a fool." [4]

He hears the chiming of the clock and knows that it is time. He strikes the match and the flame shoots out like that flame of desire in his heart. Symbolically, it catches hold and burns intensely. His liberation is at hand. But, ironically, that liberation does not come in the form of the death for which he hoped. The flames lick hungrily at his trouser leg. Suddenly he realizes that he wants more time to think. He rushes out of the shop. At that point, the flames greedily spread to adjoining buildings. In one, he believes, an old neighbor lies trapped and helpless. Dramatically, he dashes in and saves her. He is a hero, but his life is unaltered or so he believes. The fire has rid him of the business he loathes, and through the money realized from the insurance, he has achieved a bit more of the financial ease he had sought. More significantly, "something constricting and restrained seemed to have been destroyed by that fire. *Fishbourne wasn't the world.*" [5]

He decides to clear out, leaving a good portion of the money behind for Miriam. Gradually, his new mode of life leads to a rediscovery of himself and the world which now seems incredibly fresh and vital. To society, he appears as an aimless tramp with no past and certainly no future. Ironically, he is firmer of purpose than he has ever been. During his wanderings, he drinks in his new knowledge and revels in it. He discovers an inn by a river in need of a handyman, presents himself for the position and is hired. There his life expands and his goals clarify. Once he sought to end his life. Now he realizes how precious life is. He had been muddled and wrapped about as a "creature born in the jungle who has never seen sea or sky." Now he had come out of that jungle. "It was as if God and Heaven waited over him and all the earth was expectation." [6]

Like Polly, Kipps (*Kipps, the Story of a Simple Soul,* 1905) also learns the hard but profitable lesson in Wells's code of conduct. He learns that he must disregard the circumstances of his social milieu and what others hold as goals and ideals to seize that way of life best suited to his own personality. He attains happiness, like Polly, only after he realizes that he must be true to himself despite the consequences. All of his youth is clouded by the mysterious circumstances surrounding his birth. His memories of his early life are vague but poignant. He knows that his mother left him in the care of an aunt and uncle, shopkeepers in Romney, when he was quite young. Like his creator, he passed his youth in a wretched school which turned him out as ignorant and unprepared for life as when he entered. His childhood, to sum it up neatly, was bleak and unhappy, lightened only briefly by occasional friendships the most notable of which was for Sid and his sister, Ann. One day he and Ann break apart a sixpence, each keeping half as a symbol of their friendship. Soon after, she and her family move away and once again the gloom settles about Kipps's life.

He is apprenticed to a draper in Folkestone, but the new status does nothing to alleviate the dullness of his life. For several years, that life is made up of the drudgery and tedium of all shop assistants, alleviated with occassional romances which are as unsatisfying as they are short-lived. Despite the sameness of his life, Kipps yearns for something beyond what he sees for himself in the future. This yearning leads him into friendship with Chitterlow, a would-be playwright and actor. They seal their new friendship with a drink. One leads to another and Kipps, unaccustomed to whiskey and the copious amounts Chitterlow pours into him, becomes drunk. He stays out all night and, as a result, is given notice. Once again, Wells calls upon coincidence and irony for a solution to his hero's dilemma. As with Polly, whose suicide attempt is abortive, promising only a continuation of his life of misery but in reality offering him a more satisfactory solution to his problems, so too does Kipps's misfortune result in freedom.

Wells makes a point here and, in making it, draws a parallel with the events in his own life. His code of conduct is founded chiefly on coincidence. He preaches that coincidence plays a great part in life, a role other novelists like Henry James refused to recognize. Because it does, coincidence must be understood as opportunity, opportunity which must be seized as it arises. He saw the truth of his position in the circumstances on which he built his personal success: witness his own decision to give up his apprenticeship and take his chances in the world. Even his illness was good fortune in disguise. It gave him the time and the freedom to write. What had worked for him, he appears to have reasoned, must work for others provided they set aside fear for the future.

Apparently, Kipps has no other choice but to accept the situation his intemperance had precipitated. While meditating on the bleakness of his future without a position and no hope of securing one, Chitterlow, the cause of his downfall, like a *deus ex machina*, becomes the source of his good fortune. Chitterlow tells him of an advertisement he has seen for an individual named "Arthur Waddy Kipps" to whom a fortune has been left. Like a drowning man grasping at a straw, Kipps decides to answer. He discovers that he is the illegitimate son of a gentleman whose father, Mr. Waddy, refused to permit him to marry Kipps's mother. To make amends for this wrong, the grandfather has left his entire fortune to his unknown grandson.

Kipps is overwhelmed by his new-found riches. He keenly senses his lack of those social graces necessary for one as wealthy as he now is. He turns to Miss Helen Walsingham, who once taught a wood-carving class he had attended and had impressed him as intellectually superior. He soon falls under the spell of her and her family, who sense advancement for themselves. They launch him on a career of ridiculous affectation and pseudogentility for which he is totally unfit. Kipps is maneuvered into an engagement with Helen, whom he does not genuinely love. In this respect he is the emotional kin of all of Wells's protagonists, to many of whom Wells gives great intellects but denies emotional maturity. Kipps is also given over to Mr. Coote, a would-be financial expert and gentleman, and to Helen's brother who manages his wealth.

While visiting his aunt and uncle he meets Ann, who has become a servant and who is unaware of his good fortune. He realizes that it is Ann he loves, not Helen. Casting caution to the winds, he proposes to her only to be rejected. When she learns of his wealth, she demurs. Soon, however, she agrees. Nevertheless, their marriage does not bring them the happiness they both crave. True, Kipps is no longer trapped in the impoverished world of his childhood, no longer suffocated by thoughts of a future promising only drabness. But he is still restless, like Polly, sensing that the life of idleness and unconcern his money gives him is as insufferable as was his poverty. He leaves the fine house he has inherited from his uncle and decides to build another, but not the small cottage Ann wants. She desires only the simple life. Kipps, not understanding himself, also secretly yearns for it. Nevertheless, he cannot identify his yearning, so clouded is he by the conviction that he must live well in society.

Soon, the impediment is removed which prevents him from living the life for which he is most suited. He loses his fortune through Walsingham's speculations. Expecting to be plunged into poverty once again, Ann and Kipps learn that they have some four thousand pounds untouched by Walsingham. With that sum they open a bookshop which prospers enough to afford them the simple, happy life for which even Kipps now understands they are destined. But fate intervenes once again. Fortune smiles upon them in the guise of some money Kipps has loaned to Chitterlow for the production of one of his plays. The play is a huge success and Kipps's wealth is largely restored. But Kipps has learned his lesson. He no longer yearns for the ways of society, but rests content in the peaceful life he and Ann have found.

Despite Kipps's success, which is the direct result of following Wells's admonition to "damn the consequences" in pursuit of the life best suited for oneself, Wells is not like Sartre in insisting on blind struggle. There are obvious and rather calculated phases of the struggle Kipps, Lewisham, George Ponderevo, Polly, and the other Wellsian protagonists wage. Wells believed in a directed battle based on three elements which must be diligently cultivated: education, communication, and love.[7] Wells placed education above all others, perhaps because it was the means through which he achieved his own success. It could serve, he argued in his books, in the same capacity for others.

When Wells speaks of education, he does not mean formal education alone. Polly and Kipps have little and George Ponderevo just a bit more. Rather, Wells insists upon that brand of education by means of which his characters sense their own intellectual dimensions and the direction their lives must take. Like Polonius he insists "to thine own self be true." Without knowledge of self, one cannot have life. For Wells, this education can come only by "thinking hard, criticising strenuously and understanding clearly as one can . . . the general principle of one's acts." So important does he consider education of this type that he proclaims it is "of prime importance in my religion. I can see no more reason why salvation should come to the intellectually incapable than to the morally incapable."[8] And so it is with all of his characters. None reach salvation who have not submitted themselves to the rigors of the Wellsian education.

Wells attempted to develop his theories of education more completely in a realistic novel, *Joan and Peter: The Story of an Education* (1918). When the volume appeared, critics characterized it as a polemic pamphlet, treatise and tract, and called it "The New Emile," "a veritable Wells Encyclopedia," and a "hymn of hate."[9] Essentially, the work projects the idea that education might be the only means of saving the world from war and ruin. Coming as it did at the end of the First World War, there is the suggestion in it that another, still greater holocaust might erupt unless some positive concerted action is taken.

Two orphans are raised and educated by their guardians, two of whom are Lady Charlotte Sydenham and her cousin, Oswald Sydenham, who lost half of his face and all of his illusions on the battlefield. The two children are reared as brother and sister, though the one, Joan, is in reality the illegitimate child of the brother of Peter's mother.

From the outset, the guardianship results in a battle over the children's education. Ranged on one side are the children's aunts, maiden ladies who believe firmly in a Rousseauistic education essentially unconstrained by rules and regulations. On the other side is Lady Charlotte who, as is fitting and proper, understands herself as the guardian not only of the children but of England and its Anglican culture and prejudices. She secretly has the children christened against their aunts' wishes and their dead parents' will. Finally, she has them kidnapped from their school where they have been receiving a loose, free education. Peter is dispatched to a public school almost Dickensian in flavor, and Joan is placed in care of one of Lady Charlotte's dependents.

Lady Charlotte's acts are significant for Wells. He sees in them all that he hates in England—the rigid social order trying to preserve itself by imposing its ideals upon the younger generation. But he also understands the weakness of the other side. The maiden aunts represent the attitudes of the dilettantes who dabble in the new and the different but seem as powerless to enforce their beliefs on others as they are incapable of passing them on to future generations. Into the squabble steps Oswald Sydenham. A reexamination of the will which established the guardianship reveals that he should be sole guardian. A man of purpose who believes firmly in the duty of the British Empire, he determines to educate the orphans in another direction. He is determined to give his wards the opportunity to develop into adults who could prevent the horrible calamity of war from visiting the world again. He realizes that his generation, which gave rise to the Lady Charlottes and the ineffectual maiden aunts, was incapable of preventing conflict because it was lulled into complacency by implicit faith in the formulas developed in the past (suggested by Lady Charlotte's beliefs) and the hope that the false but beguiling trust in inevitable progress held by the aunts will prove to be true. The result for his generation was not progress and stability but a strengthening of those social and economic elements which can only lead to war.

Sydenham sets out to discover schools wherein the best education can be secured for his wards which would square with his beliefs. He can find none and must settle for second best. He enrolls Peter in a moderately progressive school and Joan in one of equal merit. Meanwhile, Joan is learning something of life on her own. She uncovers the fact that Peter is not her brother and proceeds to fall in love with him. Peter, however, is caught up in the fast life of London and has taken Hetty Reinhart as his mistress. Hetty belongs to the same group of Wellsian women out of which came Lewisham's Ethel, Polly's Marion, and Kipps's Helen. Hetty is pretty and superficially attractive and satisfying for only a short liaison, not for a long marriage. But Peter intends to marry her. Fortunately, he is rescued by the advent of the war Oswald Sydenham feared would come. Peter becomes an aviator and is wounded and brought down in an air battle. During his leave at home, Joan, in typical Wellsian fashion, determines to "damn the consequences" and declares her love for him. Her declaration saves him from Hetty, but not the war. He returns to the battlefield is wounded a second time and returns to civilian life.

At this point, he realizes he has gone beyond his guardian's beliefs. He recognizes them as only the first step to a broader and more valid education. He develops a higher concept than the British Empire—the World State in which all of mankind can participate and develop its true purpose, which is the salvation of the species. Oswald is caught up in his ideas. But he senses, and through him Wells seems to be speaking, that there is little time to waste in effecting that state through education. At the close of the volume, Syndenham agonizes: "Education! I have to tell them what it ought to be, how it can save the world."

But Wells, or for that matter Syndenham, was never given the opportunity to "tell the world" exactly how it could be saved through education. The novel was never developed as Wells had planned it. His publishers objected to its enormous proportions. "It is as shamelessly unfinished," he complained, "as a Gothic cathedral. It was to have been a great novel about Education." [10] While Wells had to abandon his vast scheme for the novel because of the limited vision of his publishers, he never abandoned education as a theme in his novels nor ceased to stress it as a guide to the salvation for his god-men.

He insinuates its need in his typical manner in *The Soul of a Bishop* (1917). In it he insists that man must submit himself to a special process of learning before he can embrace the Wellsian "religion" and take his place in the front ranks of his god-men. This process involves a conscious rejection of all the tenets of organized religions, to be replaced by an identification with and a compassion for suffering humanity.

Dr. Edward Scrope, after the usual education afforded to Anglican clergymen, is installed as bishop of Princhester. Slowly, his simple beliefs in Christianity are tested by the events occurring in his diocese, a small industrial town which is torn by economic difficulties. At first, Dr. Scrope calls upon his faith to resolve the problems. His efforts meet with intransigence on the part of the capitalists and impatience from the workers. Gradually, though painfully, he begins to suspect and finally reject his Christian God. But he does not reject the concept of God. His god, he discovers through his painful education, has no interest in a life after death. Rather, his deity is concerned with the future of mankind on earth. The bishop preaches the word of god, the god of things to come. The role of this new god is clearly defined. He is to bear upon his shoulders all the pains and sorrows of humanity but not for the purposes of establishing a glorious life in another world. Rather, he bears his load of pain for the glorious heaven on earth which is to come. To help this god, the bishop also preaches a doctrine of the worldwide brotherhood of man united forever against the social evils created by his own misunderstanding of his destiny. But his words fall on deaf ears. His congregation is shocked by what it hears, and he is forced to resign his position. Undaunted by his apparent failure—Wellsian protagonists seem to thrive on failure—he continues to preach the word of his god.

In an attempt to learn more about his attributes, the bishop, now merely Dr. Scrope, is induced to take a drug discovered by Dr. Dale. Its effects, similar to those produced by LSD in our own day, expand his vision of this god. He has three hallucinations, each revealing some facet of the god's nature. He is seen first as god the triumphant, the captain of mankind who has led the species to victory over itself; the second vision re-

veals to the bishop the good produced by the efforts of
men of good will all over the earth; the final vision dis-
closes the bishop's personal place in this movement
which is god in action. He learns that his place is to
preach the word of god not as one with authority of
the type he had as a Christian, but rather as one among
many of those properly disposed to the work of god.

This last vision is especially significant because, for
some time, the bishop had been led astray by Lady
Sunderbund, an extravagantly wealthy American widow
who claimed to espouse his beliefs. In reality, she is in
love with him. She hopes to use her wealth to induce
him to leave his wife and children. At first he listens to
her arguments which try to persuade him to become
the prophet and pope of a new creed. But the vision sets
him on the right course. He refuses her offer and determines that his future is to be filled with pain and
poverty for himself, his wife, and his five daughters in
order that he might preach the word of his god.

But Wells does not limit his discussion of education
to that of Joan, Peter, and the bishop. Again and again,
he reveals his interest and trust in the power of a properly conducted education. Benham (*The Research Magnificent*, 1915), the son of a schoolmaster, believes that
were he to educate himself properly, he could develop a
sound plan to rescue humanity from war, disease, poverty, and all those forces conspiring to destroy it. He believes that he has found an ally in Amanda Morris, a
brilliant girl, whose yearning for the "whole world" he
mistakes for his own yearnings for an aristocracy which
will save the world. He learns, much to his chagrin,
that her desires only embrace the London society in
which she passionately craves membership. After an
adventurous honeymoon in Europe, the couple returns
to England. Amanda succeeds in bearing Benham's child,
but loses his heart. He longs to set out on the road to

the learning which will lead to an understanding of humanity. Amanda, in the meantime, has become the mistress of Sir Philip Easton to whom Benham relinquishes her. Free of Amanda, he now sets about his travels. He visits Russia, America, India, China. Slowly but surely, what he observes contributes to a growing concept that gradually takes shape in his mind. He comes, finally, to Wells's concept of God. Ironically, before he can communicate what he has learned to the world at large, he is killed by a group of soldiers as he vainly attempts to prevent them from firing on an unarmed crowd.

Throughout the twenties and thirties, Wells hammered away at his belief in education as that force which will prevent the cataclysm which awaits mankind. Even as late as 1939, on the eve of the Second World War, Wells trumpeted the value of a proper education by demonstrating its converse. Rudolph (*The Holy Terror*) cannot undo the results of his poor education. Like the dictator his name suggests, he is as lazy, vulgar, and ignorant as the atmosphere in which he lives. He learns, motivated by his megalomania, to exploit every vile facet of human nature in order to control the people he rules. Ultimately, he leads his nation in the direction of its and his own destruction.

While education plays a large role in Wells's philosophy and in his novels, he did not believe that learning alone, even his own brand of learning, could be the sole source of that strength the individual needs to fulfill the injunction to "damn the consequences" in order to change his life and thereby save the species. He demanded that the seeker after salvation, like himself, "communicate one's thoughts to others"; to fail to do so "is a form of sin. It is a duty to talk, teach, explain, write, lecture, read and listen. Every truly religious man . . . is a propagandist." [11] And so, for that matter, is every one of his protagonists from the very first, the Time Traveller, to the very last, Albert Tewler. The Time Traveller hopes to return from his voyage of discovery to broadcast to the world the answers he proposes to discover to mankind's dilemma. The injunction to be a propagandist looms larger and clearer in *The Research Magnificent*. Like Benham of that volume, Stratton (*The Passionate Friends*, 1913), Clissold (*The World of William Clissold*, 1926), and others are burning with the desire to communicate what they have learned to the world at large.

But the need for education and communication of one's discoveries are still not sufficient forces to sustain the efforts of the seeker after salvation. Wells adds a third ingredient echoing the admonitions of the Christianity he had rejected. That ingredient is love. He tells us that the believer, if he is to effect a change in his own life and contribute to the final salvation of the species, must "use personal love and sustain himself by personal love. It is his provender, the meat and drink of his campaign." [12] He must "love as much as he can and as many people as he can, and in many moods and ways." [13] This love of man for man is the motivation for Wells's propagandists in their struggles to achieve better lives for themselves. It is this love which steels them to accept the discomforts, dangers, pains of the unknown. It is this love which forces them to reject the comforts of indecision, of conformity, of disinterestedness.

Love enters Wells's novels in two general focuses. There is the love of mankind displayed in the selfsacrifice of the Time Traveller, Benham, and others who place the interest of the race before their own. This aspect of love suggests the image Wells projected of himself as the selfless guiding light of the world. Then there exists a second focus which reflects to a larger degree Wells's personal life—the problems of love and marriage. Wells married his cousin when they were both quite young. His autobiography clearly indicates that the marriage was not contracted out of the romanticism of youth but motivated by an insatiable sexual hunger which was to plague him throughout much of his life. C. P. Snow records in one of his books a visit to Wells who was, at that time, between love affairs. Their discussion, which Snow had hoped would be of a literary bent, turned into a minute discussion of Wells's last mistress.[14]

Wells tells us in his autobiography that Isabel, his cousin, was incapable of loving him on the level and to the degree he wished to be loved. Though she could not satisfy him, he thought kindly of her. Much of his feeling for her is projected in the portrait of Mrs. Polly. There is a trace of her in Lewisham's Ethel and Kipps's Helen. What he could not discover in his own home he searched for elsewhere. While tutoring in London for the University Correspondence College, he met and fell in love with one of his students, Amy Catherine (Jane) Robbins. She was attractive, vivacious, and intelligent, much like Ann of *Ann Veronica* (1909) in her willingness to defy convention. After leaving Isabel, Wells lived with Amy and, after his divorce, they married. The marriage, however, did not prevent his pursuing and consummating his interest in a long procession of other women. Like his character Stratton, Wells held that some provision—legal or emotional—must be made for changing mates easily and permitting those who so wish to practice polygamy.

Stratton, the son of a clergyman, is an eminently successful individual who, nevertheless, is obviously deeply troubled by the events of his life which he is about to set forth in the form of an extended letter to his son. In many ways, he resembles an older Polly, Kipps, and George Ponderevo. The reader discovers that, like those characters, he is essentially restless, a dissatisfied seeker after self-fulfillment and social equity for the masses. As a member of the lower class, he yearns for liberation from the social restraints his birth has willed him. More specifically, he discovers that one particular obstacle stands between him and the fulfillment for which he yearns. In his childhood, he was brought into close con-tact with Lady Mary Christian, with whom he fell in love. He believed that because of their love they would marry. But she refuses even to consider becoming the wife of a poor man, despite her love for him. She marries Lord Justin, a middle-aged but immensely wealthy businessman, despite Stratton's entreaties. Be-fore her marriage, however, she forces Justin to agree that they would be man and wife only nominally.

Despite this agreement, which Justin later breaks, Stratton falls into despair. He volunteers and dis-tinguishes himself in the Boer War. When he returns, he is filled with belief in the Wellsian god and the destiny of the race. He also learns that Lady Mary's marriage is not successful and, when chance throws them together, Lady Mary comes to realize the depths of her love for him, the man she had rejected. They become lovers. Justin refuses to give her the divorce for which she pleads, and Stratton, who has married, cannot bring himself to part with his wife Rachel, whom he also loves. In her letters to him, Lady Mary, now the mother of two children by Justin, states the sad case of the modern woman who, though in a world pregnant with possibilities to develop one's own destiny, is still shackled by the conventions of another, less enlightened era.

Stratton is sympathetic to her pleas, having estab-lished, with the help of a rich American friend, a worldwide publishing enterprise in an attempt to live up to the Wellsian concept that every believer must also be a propagandist. But Stratton's publications do not help the situation. He can envision only one solution to the problem. That answer lies in some fundamental change in the structure and mores of society which would free a man to have as many wives as he desired. Lady Mary, however, is of another mind. She cannot continue the liaison. Those secretive meetings have become more meaningful and more important to her emotional stability, yet more abrasive to her sense of morality. She is crushed by the thought that her love for Stratton must always be fulfilled clandestinely. When Justin brings suit for divorce, a scandal seems inevitable. Driven by remorse over what it would mean to her children and her relationship to Stratton, she commits suicide.

In this novel, as in those which followed it, Wells finds it difficult to restrain himself from parading his ideas to the point where they submerge the humanity of his characters. Lady Mary's final, desperate act is almost drowned in the moralizing which it precipitates. And whole passages, including an entire chapter ("This Swarming Business of Mankind"), are devoted to outlining his private thoughts on the society of his day and the inequities it breeds. For a period of time, Stratton's altogether understandable youthful grief and pain at the loss of Mary to Justin is forgotten only to reemerge when Wells clears the debris of his thoughts and resumes an interest in the plot. The emotional problems interwoven in that plot are significant, more significant than his observations on society, because they sound a note of freedom which has become, in a sense, prophetic of that sexual emancipation enjoyed in our day. In particular, Wells's agonized cry that love does not connote ownership of another, but responsibility to him, is particularly cogent, in that it shapes to a large degree the characters of Mary and Stratton who otherwise border on caricature.

But to Wells, his proclamation of sexual liberty, coming at a period when such a decree shocked many but was welcomed by more, meant more than a device to bring his characters to life. For him it meant a release of his god-men from the bonds of sexual frustrations and all that those frustrations imply. Once permitted to fulfill their biological interests without restraint, his god-men could direct their energies to their true purposes. To be bound to a mate with whom one cannot fulfill oneself sexually is to condemn oneself to intellectual frustration and defeat. Lewisham is bound to such a one and so is Mr. Polly for a time. But women can be trapped in the frustrations and conventions of marriage as are men. Ann Veronica (*Ann Veronica: A Modern Love Story*, 1909) and Lady Harman (*The Wife of Sir Isaac Harman*, 1914) are shackled to male counterparts of Mrs. Lewisham and Mrs. Polly.

It is difficult to understand the furor and scandal produced by the publication of *Ann Veronica* in this day when no one seems disturbed or troubled by any excess which appears in print. But the England of 1909 was a very different world. Only "nice" novels were published, rarely the "trash" Wells was writing. The novel, though altered in order to achieve its publication, was vilified from the pulpit and in the newspapers as "spiritual poison" against which the malleable minds of the young must be protected. Libraries refused to have it on their shelves. Schools closed their doors against it. And, to add to the trouble it caused, it was rumored that it was a *roman à clef*. But the young bought it eagerly and loved it. It spoke to them because Ann, like Stratton, Polly, Kipps, and all of Wells's major figures, is a passionate advocate of personal freedom unencumbered, especially in choosing a mate, by parental supervision or the mores of society.

Ann is a girl who comes from a good family.

Though she is obviously brilliant and destined for better things, her father, who cannot understand her, and her spinster aunt decide that she is to have the usual education open to women of her social class. This education, essentially Victorian in cast, aims at producing in her a consciousness of the values of her class and her place in society. But Ann is dissatisfied with the narrowness of her life. In this she resembles all of Wells's protagonists, beginning with the Time Traveller. She also resembles them in her audaciousness, aggressiveness, and fierce sense of independence. This independence is manifested in her desire to go to a fancy-dress ball with the Widgetts, her lighthearted, somewhat bohemian friends. Her father's refusal precipitates a crisis.

True, some of the obstacles she overcomes seem pallid in the light of the liberties of the female of this day. One must recall, however, that the book was written in the period when women were little more than legal chattel of their fathers before their marriage and slaves of their husbands after. Therefore Ann's rebellion against the wishes of her father and her subsequent action are, perhaps, more shocking in their proper context than many an exercise of freedom performed by her sisters of this day.

Ann leaves home to live alone in London. But her hopes of making an independent living are soon crushed. There are few opportunities open to women of her class for honest work. Imprudently, she accepts a loan and the "friendship" of Ramage, a man considerably older than she. When she learns of his real intentions, she makes a violent scene. As a direct result of her disappointment, she joins the suffragette movement. A raid on the House of Commons, in which she takes part, is abortive and she is arrested. After a month in jail, she meekly returns home and accepts engagement to

Manning, a woman-worshipper who can offer nothing more to her than his protection. This sense of protectiveness she loathes most of all. He cannot understand women as anything other than childlike goddesses whose place is on a pedestal.

Meanwhile, she has turned her attention to her first interest, her biological studies. She falls in love with a laboratory demonstrator, Capes, whom she forces to ask her the question, "What do you want?" in order that she might answer, "You." Capes realizes that he loves her, but the pair cannot marry because he is already married, though separated from his wife. The decision to cast aside her promising career for the man she loves is simple for Ann. They live openly as lovers, proudly disdaining the scorn of society. The two willingly embrace poverty, for Capes has also come under the censure of society. Finally, perhaps as a plan to afford publication for the book, the couple marry, after Wells conveniently disposes of Capes's wife. The marriage restores them to middle-class respectability and to the bosoms of their families, who had rejected them. At the novel's close, Ann gives a party for her family as a fulfillment of the dream she had treasured through her long days of suffering. In the midst of her joy, a sadness overcomes her. Perhaps she has paid too high a price for the approval of society. Could that passion which drew her and her lover together retain its intensity within the prison of a conventional marriage? The question Wells proposes is significant. It saves Ann from becoming a soap-opera heroine and it points to Wells's answer. He insinuates that the passion cannot survive. *The New Machiavelli* (1911) confirms his belief. Marriage, for Wells at least, is antithetic to passion.

Lady Harman also arrives at the same conclusion, but emotionally she is quite the opposite of Ann. She is a very feminine, compliant woman who, through the events in which she plays a prominent role, begins to search more deeply into her own nature, as a true Wellsian protagonist, and by logical development turns from gentleness and docility to violence. Based essentially on the history of the suffragette movement in England, as is *Ann Veronica* in part, the novel is somewhat more than an examination of that movement. Fundamentally, it comes to grips with problems of love parallel to those probed in *The Passionate Friends, Ann Veronica,* and to a lesser extent in Wells's earlier novels. It differs in that it treats of the sexual problems of a woman trapped in an impossible marriage by her lack of knowledge of the physical aspects of love. She is like the Eloi, Weena, who cannot understand nor control her feelings for the Time Traveller. Lady Harman's problems, however, are complicated by the tawdry romantic dreams born in the poverty of her youth.

Ellen Sawbridge is a beautiful but penniless girl of seventeen when she meets and marries Sir Isaac Harman, a grasping, wealthy businessman. She sees in him the fulfillment of her wildest dreams. He, in turn, understands her only as one of his conquests equaling, but not surpassing, a business coup. Ellen has had no opportunity to learn the realities of life before she is married and the mother of four children within seven years. Harmon, though treating her as property, is nevertheless kind to her, giving her everything short of accepting her as a human with a life and will of her own. There is something extremely comic in his vast inability to listen to what she has to say and to treat her thoughts with any degree of consideration. To him she is a child, a plaything, attractive and desirable, to be placated with baubles but never to be taken seriously.

Slowly, she begins to rebel against her life. And, as her rebellion grows so grows her character, very much as Polly's grows when he begins to formulate his plans for his final escape from his constricted world. The voice of dissatisfaction swelling within her is nurtured by her interesting, but imprudent conversations with Mr. Brumley, a widower and somewhat ineffective novelist. These talks reveal to her a relationship of man to woman other than the life of pampered slavery which has been her lot. Though her friendship with him never goes beyond afternoon tea or walks in the park, Lord Harman suspects her of infidelity and carries her off to virtual imprisonment in the country. In his own way, he loves her. But his action inflames her to escape. When she does, she turns from her former romanticism to the violence of the suffragettes. On one of her escapades, she smashes the window of a post office and, like Ann Veronica before her, she is imprisoned. After her release, she forces her husband to agree to her liberty. With this liberty, she proceeds to attempt to convert him to her way of thinking. She is successful to a degree when fate intervenes. A letter from Brumley to her is intercepted by Lord Harmon. He is never in good health, and the contents of the letter cause him to suffer a stroke which brings about his death. Brumley's letter was filled with an impassioned but ambiguous statement of his feelings for Lady Harman, which Harman believed was an indication that their affair had not come to an end. At first her husband's death fills Lady Harman with an exhilarating sense of release and of coming once again into full possession of her life. When she decides to marry Brumley, it is the free decision of a woman secure in the sense of her own worth as an individual. There is something attractive in this logically developed portrait of the emergence of a personality struggling within the prison of the mores of society. Unfortunately, Wells could not see the value and ultimate reward of such a struggle when he wrote *In the Days of the Comet* (1906). That novel vitiated the need for

Lady Harman's struggle and, ironically, destroyed the joy of her victory because it postulated a world in which the frustrations of sex are nonexistent. The result is pallid, unconvincing, but eminently suitable to Wells's hope for the future.

A comet, huge and seemingly carrying destruction for the earth in its head, is sighted in the skies. The population is in a turmoil of fear. That comet, however—which suggests the loftiness of Wells's ideals—rather than destroying mankind, revitalizes it. Gases emanating from its tail cover the earth for three hours. Its green vapors overcome all living creatures and when these vapors dissipate, "Change" occurs in the Wellsian sense. Gone are the prejudices developed over the ages which have restrained mankind in its development. Gone are man's inhibitions, his fears, his foolishness. But most significantly, the suffocating sexual mores are expunged from the race. Man is now free to mate with whom he pleases without losing status in the new society which was born in those three glorious hours. Clear of the smothering effects of an outdated moral code, the species is now free to dedicate itself to the purpose for which Wells believed it was born. The salvation of the race is assured.

The story is told by William Leadford, a hearty old man. At the time of the great "Change," he was a gawky clerk in an industrial town, with woefully limited schooling, a thirst for more education, and a hatred of the privileged classes. He is engaged to Nettie Stuart, who runs away with the brilliant and wealthy Edward Verral. Leadford discovers them and is in the act of shooting them when the green vapors overcome him. At the same time a war has broken out, with England and France against Germany. The vapors also overcome the combatants.

When the men revive they discover their old enmities

have vanished, and they set about to reconstruct the world. Leadford can feel no jealousy or hatred of Verral. He senses that he should leave the lovers alone, but he returns, eventually to share Nettie with Verral. Neither has any objections to the arrangement, nor does Anna Reeves, who has married Leadford in the interim. The four join together and share the comforts of each other without discrimination or prejudice.

Despite the promise of a better future extended in the novel, Wells warns his god-men that the path to the glorious future which awaits mankind will not be smooth even with the normative guides of education, communication, and love which he established to help the individual "damn the consequences." Wells warns, as he demonstrates through his characters, that the individual who yearns for salvation "must not expect other people about you to share the consequences of your dash foward . . . You must fight your little battle in front on your own responsibility, unsupported—and take the consequences without repining." [15] The horrible dimensions of some of these "consequences" Wells outlines in his science fiction.

3

Inferno
The Science Fiction

Throughout his long career as a novelist, Wells's fertile imagination never ceased to conjure vision after vision of the hell which his god-men must resolutely confront, somewhat like Dante in *The Divine Comedy*, bravely and directly if they would be successful in the struggle for the ultimate victory of their race and the fulfill-ment of themselves. These visions are fraught with the dangers presented by a hostile nature bent upon their destruction and more intensely divisive horrors wrought by the perversities of the human species. Thus the Time Traveller witnesses the world in its final agony as the sun grows cooler and cooler. But this vision, disquieting as it may be, is fundamentally less shaking than that of a humanity degenerate and divided at war with itself. Far more crushing a horror than the cannibalism of the Morlocks is the picture of the Eloi—complacent, child-like, loveless, and deintellectualized descendants of an-cestors who had fulfilled man's dream for an earthly paradise devoid of desire, war, pain, and sorrow.

The Time Traveller's angst is no less severe, no less frustrating than that of characters such as Dr. Moreau (*The Island of Dr. Moreau*, 1896), Griffin (*The In-visible Man*, 1897), and Cavor (*The First Men in the Moon*, 1901) who, though sobered by the obstacles offered by nature to the survival of themselves and their kind, are devastated by the insights into their species presented by such obstacles. Essentially Wells understood, and these characters come to learn, that man must conquer himself before he can hope to address himself properly to the problems of a hostile nature. This is the principle which shapes and directs his protagonists. Though their struggles with forces outside of humanity are monumental, their fiercest enemy is the very nature of mankind. But, in these early works at least, Wells does not despair. Wells believed that man could achieve a victory over himself. But the reservations which clouded his hope, which he fought to control, grew ever stronger as he advanced in years and as he witnessed the manmade conflicts he had predicted. This doubt is clearly reflected in the quality of his work and the attitudes of his characters. The early, youthful, almost joyful optimism expressed in his first novel, *The Time Machine* (1895), and projected through his first hero, the Time Traveller, decays to a trenchant pessimism in *You Can't Be Too Careful* (1941) and its protagonist, Albert Tewler.

Fundamentally Wells's philosophy and creative work suggest that man's essential problem, in the light of the fact that one day he will cease to be, is the discovery of his own individuality. This is the goal toward which his protagonists struggle. The desire for individuality grows even more important as the species increases in number and tends to drown the individual in a solution the fundamental component of which is the low common denominator of conformity. The Eloi have no identity as individuals. Weena emerges from the mass only briefly. The Morlocks as well, though more aggressive, have no individuality. Wells indicates in this lack of identity that those characteristics commonly associated with identity do not contribute to individuality. The passivity, youthfulness, goodness of the Eloi and the aggressive, work-oriented lives of the Morlocks equally are incapable of shaping identity. Some other quality, obviously present in the Time Traveller, is needed to raise the Eloi from children and to identify the Morlocks as something other than animals. This necessary ingredient is explored in part in *The Island of Dr. Moreau.*

Though superficially suggestive of Kipling's *The Jungle Book*, which had just appeared (1894, 1895) and Mary Shelley's *Frankenstein*, the novel is essentially Wellsian in theme and worthy of comparison with Swift and Voltaire for its bitterness. Its satirical intent was not at first apparent, and it was read and accepted as a gripping horror story and nothing more. That Wells had a more serious intent, however, is clear from the subtitle he had originally proposed for it, "A Satire," and from the furor which engulfed him when its true meaning became clear to the public. The *Times* (London) and the *Athenaeum* denounced it as sensationalism. Others branded it indecent, and even his friends considered it in poor taste.

The doctor, a vivisector, along with his assistant Montgomery, has converted a lonely volcanic Pacific island into a zoological laboratory in which he conducts in total secrecy a series of experiments which would be condemned in England. These experiments are performed upon animals with a degree of pain almost unbearable for its subjects. Moreau's object is to achieve a perfect race of men, superior in every way to that which he despises. Pain, he realizes, is the avenue to any perfection of mankind. This is the quality Wells stresses so heavily in *The Time Machine* because he understands it as the element which defines that individuality for which he seeks. Unfortunately, Dr. Moreau's experiments have never met with complete success. He has been able only to reshape the animals into a low form of man. The delicate but absolutely necessary reshaping of the brain, however, eludes him. Nevertheless, he is not defeated by his failures. His mission is too important to admit of defeat. He goes on to produce, eventually, a whole colony of beast-men. Under his direction, they develop a travesty of human civilization, including—and this was the aspect of the book which produced the most serious denunciations of the work—a parody of religion with its ten commandments ("the Litany of the Law," the chief admonition of which is not to walk on all fours). Involved in this parody are the fear of hell, "the House of Pain," Moreau's laboratory, rules governing marriage, and a strict code of decorum. Moreau and his subaltern wage a continual and never-ending struggle to educate the beast-men and inculcate a respect for law and decency in them. The struggle is never entirely successful, for Moreau and Montgomery wage a battle against strong enemies: deep-seated animal traits and emotions, instincts and cravings which seemingly cannot be eradicated even with fearsome threats of pain and torture. Moreau's efforts to build a rational life for his charges degenerate into a mockery, a flimsy, easily torn façade behind which animal natures reassert themselves when Moreau turns his head.

Into this ironic and frustrating Eden comes Edward Pendick, a private gentleman who is the only survivor of a collision at sea. He is cast ashore on the island and finds himself an unwelcome guest. At first he is won over by the charm of the doctor and his dedication to the cause of science. However, he soon learns of the nature of the experiments when, by accident, he encounters the distorted creatures who are the results of Moreau's more successful operations. Pendick, though a student of biology, intelligent, attuned to the evils of mankind and desirous of change, immediately sides with the beasts. Their limited powers of speech and vestigial code of ethics cause Pendick to mistake them for a debased species of man. He plots to release them from what he considers the megalomaniacal control of Moreau. In the course of the plot, by accident, they taste blood. The taste enrages them and they turn on Moreau. A pain-maddened puma puts an end to him. Only after he has destroyed all that the doctor has striven for, through his misdirected charity, does Pendick realize the evil he has wrought. He returns to England only to be overwhelmed with terror when he, as perhaps Moreau before him, looks at the faces of his fellowmen. He sees intelligence in some; these are reassuring; but in many more—too many more—he sees the bestial characteristics of the creatures his flawed understanding of the situation had liberated.

Wells had several motives in shaping this volume. He wanted desperately to clarify his understanding of the fundamental character of mankind which he introduced in his first novel, *The Time Machine*. He is essentially Darwinian. Man for him is unquestionably an animal removed from the ape only by an immeasurable process of evolution and many centuries of moral training and education. All too often, unfortunately, the effects of this education and training slough off to be replaced by man's baser, more enduring instincts. The centuries have made him only superficially a rational being. Nevertheless, he possesses tremendous potentialities provided he subdue his animality. Wells outlines man's destructive qualities in all of his novels. He views complacency and comfort as the chief adversaries of man's rationality. These elements or defects of character mitigate against progress and are the basic difficulties all of his protagonists must conquer. In the same respect Wells sees the happy few, like Moreau, who fight against the *status quo*, as the champions of rationality.

These few are reflected in his protagonists who refuse to surrender to their baser natures.

Secondly, the novel was designed to draw attention to the fundamental unhappiness and confusion of much of life. Moreau's island is the world in microcosm. The beast-men, driven and tormented by a pain they cannot understand is for their own good, and by fear and by intolerable yet deliciously attractive desires, stumble through their wretched existences, never glimpsing the true pattern or direction of their lives. They are shackled by laws which seemingly do nothing but constrain their natural appetites and develop fears they are incapable of understanding. These are the elements that moved Pendick to pity and distress. Ultimately, they blinded his reason and moved him to work against Moreau, who is to all intents and purposes one of Wells's god-men. Pendick acts to release these beast-men from the very situation in which lies their ultimate salvation because he cannot grasp that all they suffer is necessary if they are to achieve that salvation which is rational life. Wells tells us that to live as a rational being is to live in pain. Like some early existentialist he proclaims the doctrine that ease and comfort is nonexistence on this plane. Pendick, misguided humanitarian that he is, gives the animals immediate release from pain and slowly they revert to what they were originally. Only too late does he realize the enormity of the evil he was wrought in the destruction of Moreau and that perfection of mankind which was within his grasp.

Wells affords no such realization to Kemp (*The Invisible Man*) as he reacts to his friend Griffin's invisibility. Like Moreau, Griffin is a scientist, a god-man, dedicated to research for the good of his species but frustrated by the inability of his fellowman to accept what lies outside of the familiar. Should any god-man like Moreau and Griffin choose to raise the species to a higher rung on the ladder of perfection, he must be more cunning, Wells warns us in these novels, than these two characters. He must be wary of the misguided within his own ranks. Pendicks and Kemps are to be found in every age.

Griffin, while exploring the problem of optical density, stumbles upon a process by means of which bodies can be rendered invisible. The formula he compounds requires a great deal of money and equipment to perfect, both of which are denied him by a society of narrow and short vision. Since he cannot afford laboratory animals upon which to test the formula for the purity of its ingredients, he must use himself. However, imperfections in the chemicals he uses cause his derangement. In desperation, he turns to Kemp, his colleague and friend. Though a fellow scientist and possessed of the ability to aid Griffin, he refuses. Kemp is the personification of the orthodox scientist, a steadfast, as Bernard Bergonzi characterizes him, "sober investigator working for his F.R.S., in marked contrast to the romantic extravagance of Griffin." [1] In terms of Wells's art, however, he is more than that. Kemp represents just one of the many flat, monodimensional antagonists Wells creates out of his insatiable desire to identify those forces which stand in the way of progress. These forces are self-satisfied, as Kemp; they are filled with a sense of their own worth, yet nevertheless, their dignity is slightly absurd. More significantly, they are dangerous because they are completely beyond the protagonists' understanding or sympathy. And, all too often, they are beyond the protagonists' control. Griffin can neither comprehend Kemp's fears of his invisibility nor the danger he presents in this incomprehension. Griffin cannot understand Kemp's lack of vision and daring, qualities he possesses in large proportions and qualities he expects to be possessed by any scientist. Nor can any of Wells's protagonists comprehend in any way other than the negative the particular forces which oppose them. They cannot comprehend because Wells creates his protagonists, ironically, as peculiarly self-centered yet intellectually gifted individuals who believe themselves interested in the welfare of the masses they somewhat paranoically proclaim to represent.

At Kemp's refusal to help, Griffin is beside himself with rage and frustration. He turns to robbery, kidnaping, and ultimately to murder, which leads to his being hunted down like an animal by a terrorized village. In the final scenes of the novel, symbolically naked, he is battered to death by the avenging mob. Only when death slowly restores him to visibility do the people realize what they have done. As Griffin's skeleton, veins, and flesh appear, the biting irony of their act is underscored. What they deemed to be a mad, inhuman creature is after all a man, vulnerable and weak as themselves.

Griffin's death serves as an object lesson to all godmen. Each, Wells warns us, must confront the consequences of his actions to better himself and the world alone, unprotected, and naked to the world. Those who expect recognition of their contribution and adulation for effort expended are only deluding themselves. No god-man can hope for such recognition nor can he expect help, even when it is logical to expect help from those of like disposition. Kemp's perfidy, like Pendick's, even though well intentioned, accents Wells's less than subtle message that mankind is not generally equipped for nor desirous of accepting the unknown. This rejection of the strange and the foreign occurs even when man has been conditioned to receive and accept what his senses and his reason deny. Thus it is when an angel (*The Wonderful Visit,* 1895) is thrust into a society accustomed to years of sermonizing on the existence of his kind.

The novel, obviously influenced by Swift's more negative postures on the despicable aspects of man's nature, is nevertheless softer and less sensational than *The Island of Dr. Moreau* and *The Invisible Man,* both of which are also steeped in Swiftian bitterness. Mr. Hilyer, the vicar of a small and delightfully attractive Sussex village and an enthusiast of ornithology is out shooting one hot summer day in hope of adding to his growing collection of birds. He takes aim, fires, and brings down what he believes to be an exceptional specimen only to discover to his horror that he has shot not an exotic bird, but a beautiful angel. As he examines the creature, whose wing has been broken by the shot, he discovers that it is not a pallid creature of the English imagination but a brilliantly beautiful "Angel of Italian Art, polychromatic and gay." Its wings throb with vivid color. It is short, thin, and beautiful in an effeminate way, and is dressed in an abbreviated tunic which leaves its legs bare.

Appalled by what he has done, Mr. Hilyer carries the angel home to treat him and house him until his wound has healed. The vicar and the angel are seen by the curate's wife and daughters, who are aghast at the evil in which Mr. Hilyer, a bachelor, appears to be involved. The angel's long hair and flowing gown suggest only one thing to them. The vicar has taken up with a woman without benefit of clergy. Wells uses this incident and the subsequent events to cut sharply and mercilessly at the pretensions of a society he abhors and a faith he feels is incapable of changing it.

He also levels his sword at the stupidity of science and medicine when he has Dr. Crump, whom the vicar has called to heal the angel, refuse to believe the evidence which his eyes present to him. The angel's wings are, in his estimation, nothing more than "abnormal growths," and much to the alarm of the poor clergyman, he strongly recommends that they be removed by surgery. Later the doctor calls the angel a "matoid," noting his (he has been established as a male) effeminate delicacy, singular mode of dress, and signs of mental weakness. These, he concludes, are obvious when the angel speaks of goodness, kindness, and fairness. Crump manages, however, to overlook all of the angel's more positive qualities in his attempt to fit him into his understanding of the real world.

Like Dr. Crump, the curate's wife and the other parishioners refuse to accept the angel for what he is. They demand that he conform to their ideals rather than they to his. Their intransigence and their fear, which he suspects lies beneath it, sadden the angel. The once-brilliant colors of his wings grow dim as he learns more and more of the attitudes of these people and the harshness of life in the world of the late nineteenth century. On every side he sees its ugliness, its pain, its disappointments. Like the Time Traveller, Moreau, Griffin, and all of Wells's protagonists, he is forced by circumstances and that great controller, chance, to confront squarely and resolutely the bitterness and unpleasantness heaped upon him. His antagonists are essentially a complacent population damned by their complacency and threatened by his nonconformity and his ideals which he dispenses freely.

The angel is forced to wear the ugly and uncomfortable clothing deemed proper for Victorian gentlemen. One concession is made, however. Holes are cut in the frock coat for his wings. Despite his surface conformity, he is forced to suffer patiently the indignities heaped upon him by the brutish village boys. Even the dogs join happily in his torture. Everyone in the village, in their almost hysterical desire to force him to accept their hypocritical concepts of right and wrong, fails to understand the quality of goodness he represents and the ideals taught by their faith which he personifies.

All fail to understand him and what he represents save the vicar, who is powerless to help him, and Delia, a servant. Delia loves him, but her love compromises him in the eyes of the village gentry. Though her love for him is the one bright spot in the angel's life, it does not lessen the mounting frustration he feels. This frustration, the harshness of his life, and the subsequent depression drain what little color remains in his once glorious wings and erase the look of rapturous joy from his face. His final degradation comes when in anger he strikes Sir John Gotch, who has accused him of trespassing, and believes that he has killed him. "Truly," he ways, "this is no world for an Angel! It is a World of Pain, a World of Death."

His release from the life he has come to loathe occurs when he dashes into a burning building to save Delia from certain death. Even this heroic, unselfish act does not move the citizenry to accept him and the goodness he represents, nor does his death in the fire broaden their vision. Wells closes the volume leaving with the reader the impression that even after so strange and wonderful experience as a visit from an angel the villagers and their gentry will continue to act with hostility and violence in the face of the unknown.

But mankind whom these villagers represent, Wells maintains, may be forced to cope with, accept, and finally come to live with the unknown. In *The War of the Worlds* (1898) he proposes that just such a situation might be thrust upon our species by a nature which has created a race superior in every way to the human. Monsters from Mars invade the earth and prepare to colonize it. At first their coming and presence are ignored. Gradually they make themselves and their in-

tentions abundantly clear. The government cannot ig-
nore them when the creatures institute a reign of terror
as they hunt humans for food. Helplessly, despite all of
man's scientific progress, his technological advances, and
deadly weaponry, his grip upon the planet is slowly
loosened. There is no Time Traveller, no Griffin, no
Moreau, no angel to offer a possible solution to the
dilemma. Nothing man does nor can do seems effective
in destroying the repulsive beings. Where, then, is the
answer to the survival of mankind? He must, Wells insists, finally and absolutely reject the fundamental posture of his invincibility and his immortality to which he
has clung in comfort for far too long. He must accept his
weakness in the face of cosmic strength to confront
boldly and irrevocably the vision of his probable demise.
In this confrontation, man must determine, despite pain
and danger and possible defeat, to arrive at new and
more meaningful formulas to govern his life upon this
planet. He must sweep away his prejudices, his parochial
vision. He must root out of his being those superstitions
which were once his comfort and his hope. He must
embrace his fellowman with the understanding that only
through cooperation can they and their species be saved.

Significantly, in *The War of the Worlds,* an unnamed
man, suggesting the typical Wellsian god-man and em-
bodying those elements in which Wells sees the only salvation for the species, devises a plan to take to the sewers
in an effort to escape the Martians. There, with the aid
of strong men with a similar will to survive and with
the necessary scientific and cultural knowledge, he hopes
to build a new life, to revitalize the species, to re-
educate it, to redevelop and redirect its values, its potentialities. Then, someday in the distant future, the
race can reemerge from its protective shelter to reconquer
what was wrested from it by a superior species.

But even if humanity is capable of surviving annihilation by a cosmic force such as the Martians, it must still confront the eventual demise of its civilization wrought by misguided nationalism and war which is its instrument. This is the message of the prophetic *The War in the Air* (1908). The novel is set in the middle of the twentieth century. Progress has come to man through the invention of the monorail which has eliminated the inefficient railroads and other discoveries of science not the least of which is the perfection of the flying machine.

Most European and Asian nations have solved the last problems standing between them and efficient travel through the air. As a result, each secretly begins to arm itself with bombers and heavily armed airships and airplanes. In the West, Germany, believing it has surpassed all other nations in its manufacture of these war machines, seizes upon a petty and little-understood quarrel with America to begin its conquest of the world.

Immediately, a fleet of armed dirigibles and protective airplanes are readied for a massive attack on New York. The "German Alexander," Prince Karl Albert, is given the command. Meanwhile in England, Butteridge, an eccentric, designs and builds a wasplike flying-machine superior in every way to any the Germans have. He wants to sell his design to his own country, but the authorities protract the negotiations by haggling over the price. Germany hears of the invention and makes it known that it is eager to buy at any price. Butterick tries to escape with his plans on the eve of the attack on New York. The balloon he uses for his flight to Germany is nearly wrecked on Dymchurch Beach and his place is taken by Bert Smallways, an out-of-luck mender of bicycles. Bert is mistaken for Butteridge and is forced to embark with the prince on the expedition to New York. His real identity is soon found out, but he is permitted to remain.

What follows is a prophetic vision of the massive bombings conducted during the Second World War.

Patterned and precise, the Germans pound New York mercilessly. Despite the massiveness of their attack and its savagery, they are unable to break the spirit of the country. Meanwhile, the news of the German attack reaches the Eastern Confederation, Japan and China, and it makes preparations to enter the war against the Germans. It launches thousands upon thousands of airplanes more cheaply constructed and far superior to those of Germany. They bomb the camp Germany has established at Niagara Falls.

In the meantime, Bert, who had been forgotten in the midst of the confusion caused by the bombing, finds himself stranded on Goat Island with all its bridges destroyed. He is soon joined by a bewildered prince and an attendant officer. The three conduct a miniature war for the possession of some food and a slightly damaged Japanese airplane. Bert kills the prince and routs the officer. He learns to fly the plane and finally takes off from the scene of destruction for England, where he is reunited with his fiancée. But no such happy fate awaits the world.

Spurred on by hysteria, the war mounts in intensity. Chaos yawns as the structure of human society collapses under the poundings of the bombs. Governments dissolve, panic seizes the people. Yet the war goes on. Nothing seems capable of stopping it. Within five years the last shreds of human civilization disappear. Pestilence and famine follow. Finally, however, the war comes to an end. The few survivors return to the broken shells of the cities to live like animals. Degenerate mankind, similar to the human beings discovered by the Time Traveller, tend pigs among the ruins.

While *The War of the Worlds* suggests that there is some hope for mankind despite the terrors it must face, and *The War in the Air* limits this hope to mere survival, Cavor's experiences in *The First Men in the Moon*

(1901) imply that even greater depths of horror await man. Though superficially reminiscent of Verne's *From the Earth to the Moon* and Swift's *Gulliver's Travels,* Wells's novel takes a different direction than either, though it is as filled with adventure as the former and as critical of humanity as the latter. In addition, it adds several dimensions to Verne's trip, making it more daring and filling it with moral implications unexplored by that author.

Cavor, a scientist, and Bedford, a journalist, journey to the moon on "Cavorite," a gravity-resisting element infinitely less dangerous to life than the power which has taken our astronauts there. It is no accident that a scientist and a writer are joined in this adventure. Wells enjoyed boasting of himself as a member of both professions. But the pairing is more significant because it suggests the roles he developed for himself in his writing. He wanted desperately to act the cool, unemotional scientist exploring the unknown. He was just as passionately dedicated to the role of the journalist broadcasting those discoveries to the world in an attempt to change the direction it is taking.

These are the functions given to Cavor and Bedford in the book. These functions shape their characters and direct their motivations. When they land on the moon, they meet its inhabitants, antlike creatures whom they name Selenites. The two are captured by suspicious natives and taken into the moon's interior. After a terrible struggle, somewhat reminiscent of that of the Time Traveller and the Morlocks, they escape. Bedford locates the sphere which carried them through space and with it returns to the earth. Cavor elects to remain despite the understanding that his decision means certain death for him. He elects to remain because he sees it as his duty as a scientist to broadcast to the earth all he observes of the Selenites. He feels that such information would be invaluable to humanity. Careless of his personal safety, so like a Wellsian god-man, and knowing that his signals will be detected, he begins his self-appointed task. He is indifferent to his fate because he is motivated by a sense of something vaster and more important than self. Polly resembles him in this respect, and so do the other major figures in Wells's more realistic fiction. But no one of these characters is confronted with a civilization quite like that of the Selenites. Only the Time Traveller could understand the disgust that is Cavor's reaction to these moon people who are, in many ways, the ancestors of Wells's Morlocks and Eloi.

They are a race who have become so specialized in the work they perform that their very bodies and minds have been modified to conform to their duties. If, for example, a Selenite is destined to do the work of a mathematician, his teachers and trainers set out at once to shape him to that end. They check any latent disposition to other occupations; they encourage his mathematical bent with psychological skill. Surgery is performed where necessary to aid them in their work. The mathematical faculties of the subject's brain grow, and the remainder of his body grows only as much as needed to sustain those faculties. In the final stages of the creature's development, except for the required food and rest, his only delight, his only interest is his mathematical pursuits. Those areas of the brain concerned with his duties increase in size until they drain all the vitality from the remainder of his body. His legs and arms shrivel; his heart and even his digestive system diminish. His features become hidden beneath the huge, bulbous contours of his brain. His voice is used only for stating of mathematical formulas; he becomes deaf to anything other than the language of his subject. He cannot laugh; he cannot feel; and he cannot love.

These strange creatures, with all their individuality and humanity bred out of them by some master planner, can no more achieve a personal identity than the ground upon which they walk. They have sold their humanity for a perfectly ordered and peaceful society. Their lives are rigidly controlled, and to that extent they are serene and unclouded by emotion or the thousand and one difficulties which plague their brothers on earth. Life in their society appears ideal. But Cavor's discoveries sound a note of warning and fear which permeates all of Wellsian science fiction. More significantly, they pose questions which must be answered in a world growing evermore crowded. Can, Wells asks, individuality survive in a century which is more advanced scientifically and technologically than any other in the history of mankind? Through his question, Wells suggests that a more horrible fate might await the species than that moment when it will cease to exist. He senses in the burgeoning of society and the increased demands on it to feed, clothe, and sustain its members an almost axiomatic erosion of personal identity. Ironically, as Cavor's attention becomes fixed on the Selenite's society, his own identity is lost. He becomes no more than a convenience which Wells uses to report his ideas.

Wells did not limit his warnings of doom to his novels. He insinuated them into his short stories as well, some sixty-three all told, most of which were written in the early years of his career when the form was reaching the height of its popularity. His first collection, *The Stolen Bacillus and Other Incidents* (1895), was an immediate popular success. Its popularity has not declined since its first publication. Though not widely reviewed, it was noted, nevertheless, as the product of a very striking imagination which, it would seem, had "a great deal within its reach." [2] The success of the first collection was followed and intensified by that of three more: *The*

Plattner Story and Others (1897), *Tales of Space and Time* (1899), and *Twelve Stories and a Dream* (1903). In 1911, a fourth collection appeared, *The Country of the Blind and Other Stories*, essentially a selection from the four preceding volumes, with several previously un-collected stories.

With the subsiding of the first great wave of popular acclaim which had erupted over what was thought to be an "unrivalled" and "audacious" insight into the literary possibilities of the discoveries of science,[3] critics began to reexamine the stories. They discovered that certain aspects of them were strikingly familiar. Several re-viewers noted elements of Swift, Verne, Poe, de Maupas-sant, Hugo, Kipling, and others in them.[4]

Wells never denied nor affirmed that he had been inspired by these and other authors, nor did he ever claim originality for his short stories or for any of the writing he had done. He was disinterested in such questions. Besides, though his critics were skeptical of his inventiveness, his audience never was. His stories were overwhelmingly popular. James and Conrad ad-mired them, and his public clamored for more. His readers sensed in them qualities not present in the tales of those to whom he is indebted. There is a sense of urgency and immediacy in his stories, a sense of danger and a sense of awe of the unknown, but above all a sense of youth and vitality projected through his use of recent discoveries of science and advances in technology. With these elements he was able to capture the exciting sense of a dawning century.

He made a pact with his readers. And in that pact, essentially a suspension of disbelief, he promised them visions of what they and their children could expect as the twentieth century opened before them. Through his predictions, based always on known fact, the future was made as clear and as meaningful as the morning newspaper. Thus he was able to predict air travel in "The Argonauts of the Air," shortly before the first test flights proved the truth of his prediction, and tank warfare in "The Land Ironclads" long before it was to come to pass in the first great war.

But his stories contain more than suggestions of technological advantages or disadvantages coming in the future. They reflect, in tightly written, hysterically intense fashion, man's innate ability to deceive himself into believing that he is safe and secure in a world and a universe that contains no safety or security for a being as fragile as he. Thus in "The Lamias," five young men confess that they have discovered that the objects of their devotion and love are nothing but an alarm clock, a phonograph, a stone that changes gold into knick-knacks, a châtelaine with keys, a bottle of perfume and a handful of busks and pads. Like the young man in the poem of a somewhat similar name by Keats, they see only what they wish to see. In a sense, these objects in Wells's story are akin to the serpent in the poem whose true form is revealed to the young man only by the philosopher who is capable of seeing below the surface of things. In this tale and those which follow it, Wells attempts to place himself in the position taken by Keats's philosopher. He desperately wants to restore to the young of all ages that clarity of vision, of perception, stolen by a corrupt society.

Despite his serious intent, Wells does not always treat so solemnly man's ability to deceive himself. There is a good deal of humor in a story, "The Triumphs of a Taxidermist," which treats of a practitioner of the fine art of taxidermy so expert that one day, filled with a monumental sense of his own worth, he boasts that he can fashion a creature so true to life that he can "beat nature." He proceeds to fulfill his boast and creates a monster that never existed but is in every way so perfect that it convinces scientists who examine it that they have discovered a new species of animal. In "The Stolen Bacillus," Wells tells of an anarchist who foolishly believes that he has stolen a vial of deadly bacillus capable of destroying mankind. This is his aim. In actuality, he has seized a strain that is harmless to humans but raises nasty welts on monkeys.

Underlying the humor of these situations is a note of seriousness. In the craftiness of the taxidermist and the evil intent of the anarchist, lies danger for humanity. In "beating nature," the taxidermist has produced a fraud which misdirects scientific enquiry. Thus the deception limits to a greater extent man's knowledge of himself and the universe so vital to his survival as a species. The action of the anarchist, on the other hand, suggests the magnitude of the evil which might be man's fate were the discoveries of science directed toward his destruction by one of his own kind. Humanity, Wells tells us, is not safe while it harbors such individuals in its midst.

But danger for mankind lies not only in the aberrations of its members, but in its very aspirations. These can be the sources of self-delusion and ultimately doom if man understands them only as the means whereby he might escape from his duties to himself and to his race. Lionel Wallace in "The Door in the Wall" is a cabinet minister whose childhood memory of a door haunts him. The door leads to an Eden-like garden filled with all the good things he has yearned for for so long but have been denied him because of his position in the world. He manages, at first, to reject the allurements of the vision, but ultimately he succumbs. He opens the door, steps through, and plunges to his death.

Like Wallace, William Hill ("A Slip Under the Microscope") is a victim of his aspirations. A passionate student of science and a product of a poverty-stricken childhood, he wishes to achieve a first in his examinations and thereby triumph over H. J. Somers Wedder-burn, the scion of a noted eye specialist whose wealth has permitted his son to progress leisurely through his education. Hill is tense with excitement on the day of the examination. Part of his task is the identification of a specimen under a microscope. The students are honor bound not to move the slide, which could lead to an easier identification. When it is Hill's turn to approach the microscope, he inadvertantly moves the slide. No one, including the proctor, notices what he has done. He is torn on the horns of a dilemma: is he to use the knowl-edge he has gained, or is he to leave the answer blank and thereby run the risk of losing to Wedderburn? After agonizing deliberation, he takes the former course. When the results are posted, his name appears first. But the victory is barren of joy. He has betrayed himself. Wracked by a conscience which refuses to permit him to believe that he would have been capable of identi-fying the specimen even if he had not moved the slide, he confesses his fault to his professor, who cannot believe that the act was unintentional. Hill is dismissed from the school, but only after learning that he would have achieved the first even if he had not answered the question. Hill's quixotic behavior based on a false sense of right and wrong has destroyed an opportunity for the world to enlist within the ranks of science one eminently capable of helping humanity.

Azuma-zi ("The Lord of the Dynamos") has also deluded himself. His delusion centers upon a firm belief that the dynamos which he cares for under the direction of James Holroyd are gods to be worshipped and placated with sacrifices. Holroyd purposely aids and abets this delusion. He is a brute whose love for whiskey is matched only by an inordinate desire to kick his "nigger help" and keep them in their proper place considerably below his own station as a white man. He resembles that segment of humanity who, throughout the nineteenth century, willingly and somewhat religiously shouldered the white man's burden, understanding that burden to mean educating and helping the less fortunate shades of mankind, but only to the point where they could prove helpful to their white masters. Ironically, Holroyd falls victim to the delusion he has fostered. Symbolically, he becomes the first human sacrifice.

But man is not merely threatened by self-delusion, as in Wallace's case, nor by the delusions imposed upon him by an unworkable and constricting traditional sense of morality, as Hill is, nor by those delusions forced upon him by other members of his species. As his knowledge of himself and the universe increases through exploration, man becomes increasingly aware that his very existence is endangered by forces beyond his ability to comprehend, no less control. Mindless though these forces may be, they seem to conspire toward one end— his destruction.

This is the lesson Besset and Vincey ("The Stolen Body") learn when they conduct an investigation into the potentialities of the human brain. Like latter-day investigators of extrasensory perception, they are convinced that man can communicate with man telepathically across vast distances. (Mind you, this is 1896). Their experiment, however, produces a strange side effect. Besset, in leaving his body, is thrust into another dimension of time wherein lurk evil powers waiting impatiently to inhabit the body he has left. This concept of evil apparently held Wells's imagination for most of his life as a writer. In his last work, *Mind at the End of Its Tether* (1945) he talks of cosmic forces at work, like Besset's evil powers, to destroy mankind from within. Alone and almost despairing in that other world, Besset's struggle to regain his body and wrest it from the evil which has possessed it is terrifying, but no less

terrifying is his discovery of countless humans like himself whose struggles to regain their bodies were unsuccessful. Fanciful as Wells's picture may be, Besset's
experiences are allegories of those terrors man will of
necessity confront as he moves resolutely to explore the
darker side of his own nature.

That very nature, Wells suggests, has willed man
terrors and fears he must come to understand and control if he is to save himself from destruction. He explores
this inheritance in "The Grisly Folk." He traces mankind's irrational and uncontrollable fears to his encounter with and struggle for superiority over subhuman
types in the dark past of man's history. Like Freud,
Wells calls for a probing of these fears despite the danger
of such exploration, just as Click courageously pursued
the apelike Neanderthal to his lair despite the certain
death that awaited him.

But conquering his shadow nature cannot save man
from certain extinction if he stands in the path of the
vast and unmeasurable powers of the universe. In "The
Star," Wells describes what might come to pass if he
does. A star is sighted in the telescopes of astronomers
who continuously search the heavens to uncover its
secrets. The star has come out of the black and un-
trackable depths which lie beyond our solar system. In
its path lies Neptune, which it destroys. Between it and
its goal, the sun, stands one obstacle—the earth inno-
cently spinning about unaware of its end. Just as innocent are its inhabitants. Men of science warn them of
the coming danger but they are unheeded, just as Wells's
warnings fall on deaf ears. Each evening, the star grows
larger and larger in the sky. A mathematician has determined that the earth is in absolute peril. No one will
listen to his pleas nor accept his computations. Only
when the star turns night into day and forces the earthly
elements on a wild rampage of destruction will man-

kind believe in its vulnerability. But it is too late. No provisions have been made for the safety of anyone. As violent storms ravage the earth and volcanic eruptions and earthquakes shake it to its core, mankind's stature diminishes to nothing in terms of the dimensions of the disaster which awaits the planet.

Man's extinction, Wells warns us, may not necessarily be wrought by cataclysmic upheavals in the universe, but by nature smiling upon another species. Such is the message in "The Empire of the Ants." Reports have reached civilization that a highly destructive species of ant has wrested control from man in the interior of Brazil. The Brazilian government dispatches a gunboat up the Amazon to explore and report upon the situation. Its captain discovers that the creatures are so highly developed and so orderly as to be capable of controlling the world while destroying man in the process. Humanity has no weapons effective against the vast army. Like the guns in *The War of the Worlds*, cannons are less than useless. Holroyd (not to be confused with the character of the same name in "The Lord of the Dynamos"), an Englishman who has joined the expedition, predicts that the ants will be masters of the world by the 1960s.

If extinction from one source or another is the fate of the fragile creature man, where then are the means to prevent it? The answer cannot come from a single individual—witness the destruction of Moreau, Griffin, Cavor, and the defeat of the characters in the short stories. Though these individuals are capable of sensing and, in some instances, of reporting the dangers which lie ahead of the species, as individuals, Wells grew to believe, they can do little more. The answer to man's salvation, Wells determined, lies in another direction which, when he discovered it, ironically spelled the end of his life as an artist.

4

Paradiso
The World State

Early in his career as a polemicist, Wells awakened to the fact that the individual imbued with a love for humanity and its future and dedicated to its preservation can do little more than achieve salvation for himself if he struggles alone. The Time Traveller, for all his display of bravery, has little effect on his species. He cannot move even those emotionally close to him. Griffin, too, though he discovers a substance which could prove invaluable to humanity, is thwarted by the very group who should have welcomed and aided him. Like him, Moreau is misunderstood and ineffectual.

By 1911, Wells in *The New Machiavelli* concluded that even the idealist in relative control of the world and thereby in a position to effect lasting and vital change can do little to alter the direction mankind is taking to its own destruction. What Wells implies is the simple fact that progress cannot be effected by an individual because of the many possibilities for his complete failure. Richard Remington, the son of a teacher of science, has had from his youth a burning desire to become a statesman in order that he might help to create a world free from hunger, war, and hatred. He attends Cambridge and finishes his studies with honors. Soon after, he marries and enters the world of politics. Some element, however, is missing from his life. Though he works wonders on the political scene, his private life grows more and more uncomfortable for him. He knows that he does not love his wife and cannot love her. He seeks elsewhere what he cannot find in his marriage. He discovers love in Isabel Rivers, a beautiful girl who did electioneering for him. She agrees to become his mistress. For a while they are happy. Then, news of his affair begins to circulate among his political enemies. He realizes that all the reform for which he has worked will be lost if they triumph. In an attempt to end the affair he goes to America, but his love is too strong. He returns, and his enemies take advantage of his weakness. They successfully block his way to the Cabinet. Remington realizes that he must make a choice: his career and all the good that he can accomplish, or Isabel. The choice falls upon Isabel. They leave England, and he lives the life of an outcast.

Remington cannot succeed because there are too many forces allied against him which he cannot conquer by himself despite his lofty ideals and political acumen. On the other hand, when the control of the destiny of the species is shared and thereby converted into a collective effort success can be assured. Individuals may contribute to an awakening of this collective effort, but ultimately it is the group which must forge ahead to achieve its single purpose.

This conclusion had a profound and a disastrous effect on Wells's art. It forced him into an essential indifference to those vital effects of character which mark one individual as different from another. After *The New Machiavelli*, he reaches a watershed in his career. Most of his protagonists become almost indistinguishable because they belong more clearly to the class of the saved, that collective body which is capable of preventing the demise of humanity. In a similar manner, all of his antagonists lose any claim to individuality they might have possessed simply because they are those who refuse to cooperate in the mission of the saved. Once Wells arrived at a successful formula of characterization which supported this enormous oversimplification of humanity, he used it over and over again, changing it slightly from volume to volume. Remington is as much Trafford (*Marriage*, 1912) as he is Clissold or any number of Wellsian figures.

But Wells's growing belief in the ineffectiveness of the individual affected his art to a greater degree. It made him more and more impatient with the conventions of the form he had chosen to convey his beliefs. This impatience is reflected in a growing indifference to story, that aspect of his work which won him so large and so enthusiastic an audience. He grew tired of intimation and allegory. He wanted to speak directly to his audience without the intermediary of character. Gradually, after 1911, he devoted larger portions of his books to direct polemic. He wanted no one to miss the points he felt compelled to make nor to misunderstand the single purpose which should motivate all of us as it motivated his protagonists.

Wells is clear in what the dimensions of that purpose are:

> First, the maintenance of the racial life; secondly, the exploration of the external being of nature as it is and as it has been . . . thirdly, that exploration of inherent possibility which is art; fourthly, that clarification of thought and knowledge which is philosophy; and finally, the progressive enlargement of the racial life under those lights so that . . . [all] may work through a continually better body of humanity and through better equipped minds, that . . . the race may increase forever.[1]

But Wells came to believe that mankind could never achieve the unity which is needed to fulfill this purpose unless a cataclysmic immolation destroys all that was, all the evil toward which man, as he understood him, was directing himself. This immolation could, as he suggests in *The War of the Worlds*, be the result of a force of nature beyond man's ability to control. This force, symbolized by the Martians, could destroy man's evil inclinations by calling them forth to battle.

Several astronomers, men of science of the breed Wells admires so, have observed strange phenomena on the planet Mars. Great flares appear on its surface. Days later, something resembling a meteor falls on Horsell Common and attracts a crowd of onlookers, journalists, and scientists. They discover, in a scene which has become almost a classic in science fiction, that the object is not a meteor but some type of huge projectile. As the crowd watches in awe, its top unscrews, revealing strange, physically revolting creatures.

The Martians, repulsive though they may be, are in every way superior to the humans who stand about dumbly observing them. They do not eat. They live by injecting the blood of animals, in this case human beings, into their bodies; they reproduce directly by the simple process of seedlike shedding of their young. They never tire; consequently, never sleep. They use "handling machines" to put other machinery together, and move about, not on legs—they have none—but in metal hoods carried on tall tripods. Their weapon is a deadly heat ray. Essentially, they are nothing more than brains and handlike tentacles. Soon they are in control of London.

Man's armies, navies, and war machines, so effective in destroying humanity, are helpless when directed against the monsters. So too are man's supernatural aspirations useless. Christianity can offer no valid answers to the reality of the death presented by the invaders from outer space. Mankind is saved by the Martians' inability to adapt to the bacteria of this world.

Yes, humanity could very well be cauterized, Wells suggests, by a natural horror beyond its understanding. But, as the war clouds gathered over Europe for the first global conflict, Wells sensed that man was not to look to the heavens for that instrument which would, paradoxically, bring with it hope for the future as well as destruction. Rather, he believed that man's twisted brain would itself plant the seeds of the cataclysm. In *The World Set Free* (1914), a relatively poor novel yet rich in ideas, he forecasts a war so devastating in its effects that it cleanses man of his evil inclinations and frees him to direct himself to his ultimate purpose to "increase the race forever."

The scene is the middle of the twentieth century. In the years since its dawning, mankind has discovered a tremendously potent source of energy by the release and harnessing of atomic disintegration. This new-found energy at first is applied to the construction of airplanes, automobiles, and other consumer goods so cheaply and effortlessly as to be available to all. The result is the complete collapse of the entire social and economic structure of society through the rapid and chaotic destruction of old industries and older moral values. Mankind, released from the burden of work under which he has labored for eons, now begins a period of degeneration, the last stages of which were witnessed by the Time Traveller in *The Time Machine*. Bored by the life of leisure a work-free existence offers, humanity turns to crimes of violence and senseless destruction. The suicide rate in America increases alarmingly. The world becomes embroiled in the effects of moral decay. Acts of licentiousness and immorality become the order of the day. Entered into with enthusiasm at first, even these fail to end the sense of boredom and frustration which grips mankind. Murder, theft, arson, and all the thousand and one acts proscribed in the past are turned to in a frenzy of desperation. Then comes Armageddon.

By 1958, the impossible situation leads to a war between the Central Powers on the one hand and the
powerful Slav Confederacy on the other. France and
England ultimately side with the latter. At first, the war
proceeds along its bloody course in a relatively conventional manner using the ineffectual weaponry and
tactics of an earlier, less technically advanced age. Slowly
the brains of the military hierarchy conceive of more
efficient means of annihilating their enemies. The war
takes to the air. Enterprising aviators, first German
then French, bring destruction to the capitals with
secretly made atomic bombs. The military leaders, however, are unprepared for the results. Once the bombing
begins, a chain reaction of explosions follows to the end
of time with only a barely diminishing intensity. Paris
and Berlin are soon piles of uninhabitable rubble
followed, within several months, by more than two
hundred other cities. The course of the war becomes
more and more intensely destructive.

Mankind, horrified by the prospects of its imminent
annihilation, turns to the saner of its leaders for help.
Leblanc, the French ambassador at Washington, takes
the initiative. He calls a conference to put an end to the
war, the cause of which by now is almost forgotten. His
call is answered by many rulers and representatives from
all over the world. They converge, almost prophetically,
upon a small town in Switzerland. A young king, filled
with a love of humanity, is the first to renounce his
powers. His unselfish act is soon followed by all the
other save for one, Ferdinand Charles of the Balkans,
the "Slavic Fox." He refuses to abdicate and turns in
anger upon the council, hoping to destroy it and its aims.
Fortunately for the world, he is destroyed by an alliance
of the peaceful nations. The council then sets about to
build a new life. Marcus Karenin is the architect of the
new world. Like the Time Traveller, he too is imbued
with a devotion to his species. He forecasts the new

civilization which shall rise on the ashes of the old. He predicts the rebirth of mankind shorn of its egocentricity, its pettiness, its hatred, through a conscious modification. "We shall go on to mold our bodies and our bodily feelings and personal reactions as boldly as we begin now to carve mountains and set seas in their places and change the currents of the winds." [2]

But for what life does this cataclysm cleanse the world? Wells's first answer, later modified, was for the life of the "Kingdom of God." This kingdom, sketchily developed in *God The Invisible King,* is the earth populated by a humanity free of those aspects of its nature which led it to the holocaust described in *The World Set Free.* In that state, mankind would be capable of pursuing its true purpose without interference.

By 1923, Wells's vision of this kingdom was clearer. In *Men Like Gods,* he describes an Eden-like existence wrought not by some supernatural being but slowly and purposefully by man himself, by all the Time Travellers, Cavors, Kippses, George Ponderevos, and Karenins throughout the existence of the species who, collectively, contributed their vision to the group who finally achieved the long-dreamed-of goal. All who inhabit that Kingdom are god-men. There are no slackers, no conformists, no damned. But, because the struggle to delay mankind's ultimate demise is the avowed purpose of each individual, there is no pain. No one is called upon to sacrifice his life like Moreau. No one will be destroyed because of his scientific discoveries like Griffin, nor made a pariah, like the angel, for his spiritual ideals.

Mr. Barnstaple, like Wells, inhabits a world—that of the present—in which his yearning to save humanity and his unselfish devotion to it are scorned by his fellow creatures. He is a journalist and humanitarian who becomes increasingly ill at ease with the narrow concepts of nation and nationalism. As an internationalist, he understands that mankind can be saved from the second global war he senses is coming only in a community of peoples all clearly and irrevocably dedicated to the preservation and perfection of life on earth. In this and other proclivities, Barnstaple closely resembles in all save one respect the entire list of Wells's protagonists who preceded him. He is as predictable and colorless as the formula from which he draws his being. In Barnstaple, Wells cast aside any desire to breathe life into his characters; gone are the little touches of humanity which brought to life Kipps and George Ponderevo. Even the relatively flat Time Traveller is vitalized by his aura of youth and idealism. But what is admirable in him—his questioning and restless spirit—in Barnstaple becomes petulancy and prejudice.

Barnstaple is oppressed by the contemporary scene, the world of the 1920s. The war to end all wars was officially concluded just a few short years before, but its effects and those causes which precipitated it are very much in evidence. The cancer of bitterness and the disease of wounded national pride cloud the air and point to the coming of an even more devastating holocaust. Barnstaple knows that mankind has not profited from its cauterization despite all that he and others of a similar mind have done to build a rational world on the destruction left by the war.

Finally he arrives at what he realizes is a crisis in his personal life. The burning hope for the future he has nurtured within him seems doomed to suffocation by his depression. He realizes that he is on the sharp edge of a nervous collapse. Leaving wife and family, he takes an extended holiday in his motor car. Meanwhile, two scientists who have been delving into the problem of the time-space continuum, unknown to them, focus their experiments on the general area through which Barnstaple is driving. Suddenly and unaccountably, he discovers that he has been transported to another world which occupies the same space as ours but in another dimension. Two other groups in cars cross at the same time.

The world they enter is one of which Barnstaple has dreamed all his adult life. It is a utopia peopled by individuals so perfect and so wise that all live in harmony, and so virtuous that, like Adam and Eve whom they resemble, they go about naked. Disease and poverty are unknown, long since ended by the collective efforts of an enlightened race. Society is firmly based on five principles of organization: Privacy, Free Movement, Unlimited Knowledge, Free Discussion and Criticism, and Truthfulness, with Lying the primary crime. Monetary systems have been abolished; government is vestigial. No politicians exist and no peasants, but many millions of scientists all working to extend the life of the species. Speech is unnecessary, since the powers of telepathy have been developed. And, of course, there is no form of marriage tolerated. Free association is the rule. Each may mate with whom he chooses. This freedom in love, long advocated by Wells in his novels, lends dignity to the individual. Woman is not man's subject but, more significantly, man as a consequence is no longer inhibited in his life's work by jealousy, passion, anger.

But the perfection of this world is not without a flaw. The other groups which crossed the time barrier with Barnstaple are not so fascinated by this utopia. Led by Mr. Catskill, the secretary for war, they embody all of Wells's pet hatreds. In the groups are the Catholic priest who rails at a church and marriage-free society; the statesman who sees degenerate weakness in the peace and harmony of the utopians; the philosopher who continues to spin out ponderous arguments for the very existence which is theirs; the aesthete incapable of perceiving true beauty.

Fortunately, the utopians sense their vulnerability to the insanities of these men and quarantine them lest the infections spread. Forgetting for once their mutual antipathies, the members of the group unite in common cause to destroy the utopia. They become the snake in this Garden of Eden. Only Barnstaple resists them and when, to save themselves, the utopians return the group with him to his own time, he is the only mourner.

There is a multileveled irony in this novel, some of which escaped Wells's understanding. It hints at the ultimate depression Wells was to suffer in the closing years of his life and suggests the nature of his failure as a novelist. This irony emphasizes one aspect of humanity's paradoxical position which he consistently refused to face squarely and honestly. Not only was Wells incapable, as was Barnstaple, of remaining in the Eden his imagination and desire created, but he was also incapable of understanding the action of the group in attacking the utopians. They attack the peace and serenity for good cause. They do so because in a sense they represent man as he really is, a creature filled with foibles, torn by dissension, pettiness, and the thousand and one shortcomings which make the extended peace Wells hoped for impossible but more significantly, intolerable. Wells's hatred for their vices extends to a hatred for them. This is his chief failure. He does not love his characters, because he refuses to understand them. This lack of understanding forces them into flat caricature. The utopians, on the other hand, suggest another aspect of mankind. They represent his lofty aspirations which, though essentially unattainable, make life bearable for so cantankerous a species. Without a hope of some future perfection, man has no purpose, no drive to project him through and beyond his flaws and his failures. These aspirations, nevertheless, can never be fully realized. They are guides, not patterns for life, and they exist in all of us—the evil creatures Wells so loved to castigate as well as the good. Wells could never grasp this mélange which is the nature of man. Nor was he completely capable of understanding the nature of the change man must undergo were he to achieve a life of peace and perfection.

Wells did, however, dimly recognize a need for a radical change in man. There is a hint in Karenin's prediction of biological change. The earlier novels, however, were too confused by a desire for social egilatarianism to confront the problem directly. There is, nevertheless, a tone of melancholy and pessimism which pervades these works. This tone or mood suggests that Wells, even when at the apogee of his optimism, knew that no leveling of the social classes could fulfill his dream of a better life.

The Time Traveller's encounter with the Eloi emphasizes the point. Here are creatures singularly free from care and social cast, childlike in their innocence, beautiful in countenance and thought. Yet they are as fundamentally repulsive as Barnstaple's utopians. They are not human. They have no faults and hence no real definition. As unattractive as the concept may sound, man's faults characterize him more genuinely than do his virtues. Wells failed to understand that empathy is established between character and reader by the reader's recognition—rarely conscious—of his own foibles in that character.

Wells came close to an understanding of this principle when he wrote *When the Sleeper Wakes* (1899; reissued in 1910 as *The Sleeper Awakes*). Graham discovers the paradox much to his regret. Like Barnstaple, he is conveyed to another world. Unlike him, however, Graham's conveyance is not the sophisticated experiments of twentieth-century scientists, but a lethargic sleep similar to that of a prince in a fairy tale. The analogy is not far

from wrong, for Graham in a Wellsian sense is a prince
and his story is a fairy tale. He is a socialist who yearns,
even in those early days, for a world much like that
discovered by Barnstaple. During his long sleep various
fortunes become his through inheritances of descendants
who have died. These and the compound interest which
they gather make him virtually the owner of the world.
His property, because of his inability to administer it,
is controlled for him by a council of trustees who become the real rulers of the world.

They institute what appears to be a utopia. The world
has become a marvelous place where all the evils emanating from the uncontrolled capitalism of Wells's world
have seemingly been eliminated. Family life has disap-
peared, replaced by day nurseries and automatic restau-
rants reminiscent of the Horn and Hardart chain. There
is no countryside, which has long since been absorbed
by a burgeoning population. In its place are huge,
windowless, centrally air-conditioned buildings. Traffic
in this monstrous complex is controlled by a series of
moving sidewalks and intercontinental trips are made in
huge airplanes. There are no wars since all the needs of
the population have been provided. All of the enervating vices which have held man's greatness in check
for thousands of years are apparently removed by psychological treatment. Freed of hatred, pride, and sensuality,
society can be ordered and controlled by a central group.
But even in this beautiful world a flaw exists. One vice—
Wells's only concession to humanity—though seemingly
controlled, cannot be eliminated. Its seed takes root and
blossoms in Ostrog, a politician eager for advancement.
His greed for power incites the uneducated, but ma-
terially satisfied workers to revolt.

He knows that he can achieve his desire—control of
the world—only if he can become the guardian of the
Sleeper, as Graham has come to be called. After some

experimentation with stimulants, Ostrog manages to wake Graham from his 203 years of sleep, and then proceeds to manipulate him to his own ends. He plays on Graham's naïve and somewhat touching awe of mankind's technological progress. With a particularly human touch which Wells seems to have lost in his portrayal of Barnstaple, Ostrog proceeds to mold Graham through Graham's chief interest, sportsmanship. He amuses and beguiles him with the delights of flying and, appealing to his basically puritanical nature, Ostrog helps him to explore the scientific and social advantages of a world which is seemingly fresh and new. Graham falls into Ostrog's plans and willingly follows his directions. Once again, in a figurative sense, Graham has fallen asleep. Beguiled by Ostrog's words, Graham's life falls into a placid pattern as meaningless as those decades of his deep sleep. Slowly, however, he becomes aware of an element missing from the life to which he has wakened. Like all Wellsian heroes, he feels the need for love. And love comes in the form of Helen Wotton, Ostrog's niece.

Beautiful and intelligent as Ann Veronica, as dedicated to just causes as Lady Harman, Helen knows what her uncle is attempting to do and pledges her very life to thwart him. Like the true Wellsian heroine, she uses Graham's love, which she reciprocates, to open his eyes to his duty to the masses who have longed for his awakening. At this point, the novel becomes a tract. Seemingly no longer interested in the human implications of the interesting situation he has created, Wells begins once again to beat the drums of his faith. Graham comes to realize that he must lead the less well endowed masses to a true utopia—that heaven on earth of Wells's dreams—of which their present life, though materialistically comfortable, is only a shadow. Graham preaches the word of man's perfectability and turns on Ostrog and the forces he controls. The battle is fierce and bloody, but the reader senses that victory awaits the forces of good.

Though Wells, through Graham and other characters, insisted that mankind can achieve a perfect earthly existence by the correct application of his talents guided by the Wellsian faith, he understood unconsciously that the race cannot completely and absolutely control its own nature, the key to that achievement. It was years before he completely accepted the truth of mankind's dilemma, and when he did, he could not apply that understanding to an enrichment of the literature he produced. Rather, he lost all hope for the future and his characters lost the spark of life.

But Wells was far from despair when he wrote *Men Like Gods*. Its utopia could, he believed, be developed through man's ingenuity, provided he learns to cooperate with and adapt himself to the discoveries of science. Wells welcomed those discoveries but he disregarded the shattering effect rapid scientific advancements have on a patterned society and inherited ideals. For Wells, the scientist was not a destroyer of the past, but a purifier. His understanding of the significant role of science in developing his leaders—now not god-men but "Samuri" —who could fulfill his dreams for humanity is described in a delightfully humorous, but basically serious novel, *The Food of the Gods* (1904).

Bensington and Redwood, two scientists, discover and manufacture Herakleophorbia, popularly called "Boom-food," the food of the gods which has the amazing property of stimulating growth five to six times the normal. Some of it finds its way by accident into a stream and turns a seemingly innocent and charming English pond into a chamber of horrors. Redwood feeds some of it to his boy. It is also fed to other children including the infant Princess of Weser-Dreiburg. Their enormous and rapid growth shocks and ultimately threatens those of normal size, for the food not only stimulates the growth of the body but causes dramatic growth of the intellect as well. These giants, at first awed and ashamed of their size, soon begin to sense the power for good which is theirs by reason of their infinitely superior intellects. Hampered and restricted on every side by the smaller and less gifted, they are hounded into retreating from the society of their fellowmen. A politician begins violently agitating against the food and for "the preservation of normal proportions."

Events come to a crisis when Catherham, the politician, has succeeded in frightening the populace to the point where he manages to capture an office at a general election. He attempts to prevent the young Redwood, now a fully grown giant, from meeting the giant Princess of Weser-Dreiburg knowing full well what such a meeting might produce. He senses that they will fall in love. He fears love, especially between these two most gifted of the giants, because he knows when love comes it will bring in its wake the final defeat of the smaller people he controls. But love, as in all of Wells's novels, is too strong a force to be thwarted. The two giants meet, fall in love, and resolve to join the colony of the other giants who, after Catherham rejects their proposal for peace, prepare for the inevitable war between the great and the small.

Though laced with comic implications—there is a delicious scene in which one of the giant babies overwhelms his normal-sized mother, who continues to treat him as if his proportions were also normal—the essential seriousness of the novel's allegory shines through. Science, Wells claims, is not always aware of the consequences of what it discovers, especially as those consequences affect the direction of the relationships of human to human. These discoveries, nevertheless, are important to the perfection of the race despite the enormity of the problems they present to mankind. Man more often than not rejects the results of scientific investigation. Yet, ironically, the work of the scientists will ultimately elevate the species. But this elevation, this upward movement toward the goals for which Wells longed, can be accomplished only by a small group who discover their own strengths and with the help of science use them to a good end.

During the teens and twenties of this century, Wells raised up a whole crop of giants in his novels like those herakleophorbites and consequently, was perhaps the first novelist of the century to probe the human implications involved in a world growing more and more oriented to the rapid changes in long-established patterns of living wrought by scientific discoveries and technological advancement. The "food of the gods" upon which this new crop of giants was nurtured was the heady freedom granted to the lower classes by those discoveries and those advancements. These new giants were the Ann Veronicas and the Lady Harmans who fought for the freedom and the equality of the sexes and shocked the reading public by their boldness; the Traffords and the Strattons who explored the growing and changing dimensions of marriage in this twentieth century; the Britlings and the Job Husses who searched for meaning and stability in a world growing ever more meaningless and unstable. And there are the Clissolds, the analyzers and architects of man's redemption.

But Wells was never content to remain within the novel to achieve his ends. He grew more and more restless with the form as his convictions concerning future catastrophes for humanity grew clearer and clearer. Moved by the knowledge that he must act with haste if this world is to be saved—he wrote in *World Brain*, "in the race between education and catastrophe, catastrophe is winning"—he turned petulantly from the novel to issue reams of directives to mankind without the benefit of a beguiling story. He wrote about war and its consequences (*The War That Will End War*, 1914; *The Peace of the World*, 1915; *What is Coming, A Forecast of Things After the War*, 1916; *The Elements of Reconstruction*, 1916). But closest to his heart he wrote of a community of nations which would end war forever (*In the Fourth Year*, 1918; *British Nationalism and the League of Nations*, 1919; *The Way to a League of Nations*, 1919). And he wrote of the future (*A Forecast of the World's Affairs*, 1928; *The Shape of Things to Come*, 1933).

But his mind was preoccupied with the past as well as with the present and the future. He saw in his examination of history a pattern which supported his understanding of humanity and his ideas for the salvation of mankind. His preoccupation resulted in a monumental, if somewhat tedious and less than factual *Outline of History* which began to see the light of day in 1920 and took its final form in the hands of editors in 1961, long after his death. In it, Wells imposes a general thesis upon all the events in the life of the species. These events, he held, are reflections of man's intellect attempting to control and direct his race so that his "life . . . forever young and eager, will presently stand upon earth as upon a footstool and stretch out its realm against the stars." [3] This burning hope for mankind soon turned to ashes.

5

Apocalypse

The forces which moved Wells to write—his love for humanity and his fear that it would one day cease to exist—were emotionally never far removed from the events of his own life. Earlier we saw how the vicissitudes of his youth were distilled into the substance of his first novel, and the facts of his intellectual and emotional growth into his subsequent works and theories. In the early phases of his career, his novels were greeted by an enthusiastic public. His popular success was reflected in his growing optimism, in his belief that man through a concerted effort can effect his own destiny. As he grew older, and the ideals of his youth were not fulfilled, the note of pessimism which was never totally absent from even the most optimistic of his works grew louder and louder. He began to doubt the efficacy of even the most well intentioned individuals to change the world by themselves and called for collective action. Tragedy began to cloud his personal life. His second wife, to whom he was most devoted despite his adventures with other women, was diagnosed as having cancer. Fits of depression overcame him as he helplessly watched the disease lay waste her frail form. That same enervating sense of impotence is reflected in the work he produced in that period. As she drew closer to death, his fits of depression increased, but a certain peace came into their relationship. Gone were the memories of the many violent quarrels that they had had over his many love affairs, all replaced by a peaceful resignation. She died in 1927, and with her death came emotional problems which all but overwhelmed him. The extent to which these problems controlled his ever-deepening depression awaits a more detailed and definitive biography to explore.[1] Despite the absence of such a work, it is safe to say that her death and the short, uncomfortably turbulent love affairs which followed contributed nothing to Wells's emotional stability.

In the seventh decade of his life, death must have seemed but a whisper away. Nevertheless, an approaching death and emotional disturbances cannot completely account for a collapse of hope in Wells's declining years. Some other, more fundamentally disturbing element must be blamed. By 1930, the flood of novels which had enchanted the public had almost come to an end. Wells had more or less dropped the cloak of fiction to disseminate his ideas. As a consequence, his popularity suffered even though his earlier, more saleable work, which he considered of little importance, had a wide and ever growing market. In 1933 two new collections of these pieces, *The Scientific Romances of H. G. Wells* and *Stories of Men and Women in Love* were eagerly bought. Some of these pieces were equally popular as motion pictures.

Coupled with his failure to retain an audience which was once hungry for all he wrote is the fact that Wells sensed the impending disaster of the second world conflagration which all of his exhortations and advice seemed powerless to prevent. He saw in Mussolini's control of Italy and the rise of Hitler in Germany the seeds of the holocaust he had predicted in earlier works. In 1927 he wrote a short, barbed pamphlet, *Playing at Peace*, in which he chided the world for the inadequacy and hypocrisy of contemporary peace movements. The year after, he produced Mr. *Blettsworthy on Rampole Island*, "a caricature of the entire world of humanity."

Mr. Blettsworthy, obviously Wells himself, the only representative of sanity in a world gone mad, is shipwrecked, symbolically, on an island suggestive of the world of the third decade of the twentieth century. He finds himself the captive of a lunatic tribe of savage cannibals who, rather than destroy him, permit him to live among them as a sacred madman. Thus Wells saw his own position in the world. The laws and the customs of the island are sharp, Swift-like caricatures of those of civilization, and the people who inhabit it are reflections of his pet hatreds. But Wells saves his most biting comments for the Megatheria, the giant sloths, which abound on Rampole Island. These huge, ungainly, and loathesome creatures suggest those basic human institutions against which Wells had fought all of his life: the state, the church, the army, the law. The Megatheria suggest these institutions because they refuse to adapt to present realities. But, despite their ungainliness, the giant sloths are pictured as powerful and cunning adversaries possessing instinctive skills for self-preservation.

Eventually, the island goes to war over an obscure and little-understood tribal dispute which is inflamed beyond its importance. The natives are plunged into a war hysteria despite Blettsworthy's admonitions for rationality. Blettsworthy, and through him Wells, uses the senseless war to draw an unfavorable comparison between the stupidity of the savages and the equally idiotic actions of a supposedly civilized Europe. Despairing of ever changing the attitudes of the inhabitants, Blettsworthy contrives to escape from the island. Suddenly, he discovers himself in New York where, through psychoanalysis, he comes to believe that his adventures on the island were merely figments of his overactive imagination. He concedes that this must be the case despite his intense and somewhat painful memories of the barbarities he had witnessed. Finally, he concludes that Rampole Island was only "the real world looming through the mists of my illusions."

He is conscripted into the army and sent to the battle-fields of France. He records a passionately moving account of trench warfare and, in the midst of the account, he comes to the realization that he has never left Rampole Island, that Rampole Island is the world. Wounded, he returns disillusioned and depressed to England where he attempts to pick up the threads of his life. But his days are haunted by the recollections of the cruelty and the insanity he has witnessed. The world of reality slowly gives way to visions of the Megatheria, the savages, and the island's military chiefs, now more powerful than ever. He is shaken by the enormous fund of evil unleashed by the Great War and such disquieting events as the execution of Sacco and Vanzetti in the United States. Terrorized by thoughts of the evil and the conflicts awaiting mankind in the future, Blettsworthy closes the volume with the record of a long conversation with his friend, Graves, which is filled with his fears and the ever-recurring and ever-haunting vision of Rampole Island.

Mr. Blettsworthy on Rampole Island is an interesting volume because it is more clearly indicative of Wells's understanding of the world than any of his previous works. It is also an important work because it affords insights into the craft he practiced. Here one alone, Mr. Blettsworthy—a thin alias for H. G. Wells—is possessed of that rationality necessary for a proper course in a society composed of madmen who, because of their madness, cannot judge the morality of their actions. The sense of frustration, of angst, with which Blettsworthy must learn to live is not a new note in Wells's work. It is present to a limited degree in all of his characters: in the Time Traveller who must contend with the insensitive Elois and the voracious Morlocks, in George Ponderevo ill at ease with his uncle's success, in Cavor as he examines the Selenites. But Blettsworthy's angst is another piece of cloth more akin to that endured by Kafka's protagonists than to the creations of Wells's early years. The Time Traveller, Kipps, Mr. Polly, George Ponderevo were produced by a vigorous and a young mind for whom the future was promising. They are imbued with that trust in progress based partly on the implications of Darwinism and technological progress of the late nineteenth century and grounded in the idealism which is youth. Blettsworthy, on the other hand, is modern man marooned on an uncharted island alone in the sea of humanity, misunderstood by an uncomprehending populace, and without a frame of reference to lead him out of his dilemma. There is no hope for him. *Mr. Blettsworthy on Rampole Island* is a hopeless novel because Wells was without hope.

In 1934 Wells visited Stalin in the Kremlin. Wells had been, like many socialists, enchanted with the Soviet experiment. To him, the state erected in Russia on the ruins of its empire came closest to resembling the dreams he held for humanity. By 1920, however, when Wells visited Lenin, the disenchantment had begun. He began to see in Russia not the fulfillment of his dreams, but a fulfillment of his nightmares, the same bad dreams which haunted his utopias. Here was the world of *When the Sleeper Awakes* and *The First Men in the Moon*. Like Cavor, Wells observed the workings of a state moving toward that specialization he sensed was a threat to man's humanity. The visit with Stalin did nothing to reassure or comfort him. He was appalled by the rigidity of the application of Marxist ideology. What was to have been a forty-five-minute conversation developed on Stalin's insistence into a three-hour debate.

Wells upheld the concept of a world citizenry dedicated to the good of humanity—the idea he had postulated in his most recent books—and Stalin, like Ostrog, pounded away at the theory of absolute control resting in the hands of a dictator. The fruitless meeting served only to deepen Wells's growing depression. Hitler in Germany, Mussolini in Italy, now Stalin in Russia, America in the throes of a depression engulfing the remainder of the free world, and the men in power everywhere indifferent to peace and the ever-pressing needs of a humanity crying for help—this was the picture he saw.

As mankind ticked its way to the doom of a second world war, Wells threw himself back into his work in a vain attempt to stem the tide. He produced his autobiography (1934)—a summation of his contemporaries, his early life, his aspirations—and *The Anatomy of Frustration* (1936), a detailed account of his later years which he called an "interview with himself." He turned his hand to the films with which he began experimenting in the twenties (*Bluebottles, Daydreams,* and *The Tonic* for Anglo Pictures), hoping to reach a wider audience. He wrote the scenario for *Things to Come* (1935), a prophetic work about a world destroyed by war, and *The Man Who Could Work Miracles* (1936), concerning an individual who, granted the gift of having every wish come true, pleads with the powers who bestowed the gift upon him to return him to his powerless state. In the film, Wells underscored the futility of a single individual's attempts to save mankind from self-destruction.

In *Idea of a World Encyclopedia* (1936), he reiterated the theme of collective action by proposing a pooling of man's knowledge to be made readily available to anyone interested in helping humanity. *The World Brain* (1938) developed this concept a step further by advocating an organization of all libraries and information services into one integrated international system with up-to-the-moment information in a form accessible to anyone.

Despite the positive cast of the proposals he embodied in these two works, he sensed the fundamental ineffectiveness of his ideas. He knew instinctively that he was incapable of directing the world away from the doom of a second world conflagration. That the war would come, he was certain. *The Autocracy of Mr. Parnham* (1930) reflects that certitude. The novel describes the ability of a demagogue to lead even the most intellectually enlightened down the path to a devastating war. Finally, on the eve of the war Wells predicted, he produced *The Holy Terror* (1939), essentially the anatomy of dictatorship in which he describes the role that a poor education, an atmosphere of moral laziness, vulgarity, and above all, an indifference to the needs of humanity —in short, the forces against which he battled all of his long life—play in the formation of that instrument of mankind's doom.

The novel tells of a tiresome, ill-tempered boy—a holy terror—who, in earlier books, would have been an object of comedy. Wells gives the child a social failure as a teacher who hopes, through his charge, to wreak vengeance on the world that has disregarded him. Carefully, he nurtures the child on hate and, just as he is to triumph, the boy, now fully grown, turns on him and destroys him. Rudolph (obviously a play on the name Adolph) goes on to bigger and better conquests. Carefully, and rather skillfully, recalling somewhat the skill with which he constructed the psychological portraits of George Ponderevo and Kipps, Wells depicts how Rudolph, narrow-minded though he is, is able by concentrating on a few simple ideas and giving free play to his brutality, to win his nation to his madness.

But Rudolph is not totally to blame for the catastrophe he causes. Wells is clear on this point as he carefully evaluates those forces which paved the way for Rudolph's victory. Like a repetition of all that he produced to this point, he lists the attitudes he had never ceased to condemn. There is the individual who takes advantage of the moral confusion in his country to pave the way for his own material gain, the military chief who senses in Rudolph's accession to power his own personal victory, the nondescript who hope to settle their petty quarrels under his banner. All contribute to his rise as dictator. In tracing this rise, Wells analyzes the victory of the Nazi party in Germany, though he sets his book in England. Rudolph begins by appealing to the base instincts of the man in the street, flattering the underdogs, and offering cheap, simplistic plans for the correction of complex civil problems. He exploits social snobbery and vanity. Finally, with the help of a traitor, Rudolph gains control of the English Fascists and is on the road to the destruction of the world.

The war years brought with them three works negligible as art but significant as reflections of Wells's state of mind and his attitudes toward his writing. He produced two novels (*Babes in the Darkling Woods*, 1940 and *You Can't Be Too Careful*, 1941) and a long essay, *Mind at the End of Its Tether* (1945). The first is an abortive attempt to produce a second *Mr. Britling Sees it Through* (1916). Britling was Wells's answer to the First World War and all the dangers man must confront with courage and hope in the future if he is to perfect himself. He is a prosperous man of letters, like his creator, with a passionate interest in and love for mankind. After years of struggle he has achieved a life of relative ease at his house in Essex. He has had a stormy emotional life with his first wife, whose son Hugh is his chief attachment, and with his second who has long fallen from the rank of mate to that of a pleasant companion and housekeeper.

But the outbreak of war in 1914 has put an end to his comfortable existence. At first he refuses to believe that the Germans pose any real threat to England. His deep-rooted faith in the sanity of mankind is unshaken. Slowly, however, he comes to realize that his faith has been founded on shifting sands. He turns into a violent denouncer of the German mentality that has brought humanity to the edge of chaos. He attempts to enlist, only to be rejected. His son, Hugh, is more successful and is dispatched to the front. His vivid letters describing the sordid brutality of war depress his father and his death shocks Britling beyond belief. Torn by his son's death, he resolutely vows to dedicate himself to changing mankind so that the death of his child and countless others will not have been in vain. He recognizes the stirrings of a new consciousness among men of good will, men like himself who are becoming aware of their common brotherhood and understand that the waste of young lives on the battlefield is the price which must be paid for a new and a better world. *Babes in the Darkling Wood* weakly and unconvincingly echoes this sentiment. Stella and Gemini, though younger than Britling, have not an ounce of the hope which filled him. They are young only physically. Their imaginations and aspirations are old and feeble.

Like Stella and Gemini, Albert Tewler (*You Can't Be Too Careful*) is reminiscent of an earlier, sturdier figure. He is as spiritually and emotionally emaciated as Albert Polly. Unlike Polly, however, he is not possessed of that determination to alter his life, to "damn the consequences" which moved legions of his fellow protagonists. Tewler, like Wells in his seventy-fifth year, has no place to go, nor does he seem to desire a destination. He is the product of the haphazard, misdirected education of so many Wellsian characters, and he is as incapable of adjusting socially as he is incapable of enjoying himself sexually. His only answer to his problems is to remain as he is. For Wells, Tewler is a picture of the English on the eve of the greatest test of their strength that they have had to endure in their long history. He believed that they would fail.

That Wells's deposit of hope was overdrawn is more than evident in *Mind at the End of Its Tether*. The book preceded, but only shortly, the dropping of the first atomic bomb. "Our universe," he writes, "is not merely bankrupt; there remains no dividend at all; it is not simply liquidated; it is going clean out of existence." [2] He had become obsessed with the war. Despite the pleas of family and friends, he remained in London during the worst of the blitz. Once a bomb destroyed a neighboring house. The event served only to add fuel to the anger which burned within him. He was angry at the abysmal stupidity of the war and worked unstintingly to discover the means to end it. He saw in the Allies' demand for an unconditional surrender the prolongation of a conflict which had already lasted far beyond the limits of human endurance. To continue was not to end the possibility of a future war, but to guarantee that it would occur. It was in this context of anger, frustration, and hopelessness that *Mind at the End of Its Tether* was born. Only thirty-four pages in length, it nevertheless summed up his life's work. He found that work wanting. He realized that he was in no way effective in ending chaos. The Antagonist, the name he gave to the hostile forces abroad in the world, had triumphed. Wells left a final message developed out of his growing conviction that man's worst enemy was man. "The human story has already come to an end . . . and Homo Sapiens in his present form played out . . . The stars in their courses have turned against him and he has to give his place to some other animal better adapted to face the fate that closes more and more swiftly upon mankind." [3]

Beneath the horror of the war, rapidly declining health, and a series of emotional difficulties lies yet another and perhaps more significant cause for Wells's depression. This cause questions the very hypothesis to which Wells dedicated his life. It reduces to nothing his scores of books, his popular success, the adulation of which he was the object for so long. Early in this century when Wells was formulating his dream of altruistic god-men motivated by a consuming passion to forestall the death of the species they loved so much, he sowed the seed of the despair which darkened the last twenty-five years of his life and devastated his art. That seed lies in a pronouncement he made in *First and Last Things* (1908). He tells us "one's entirely separate individuality is one of the subtle inherent delusions of the human mind." [4] In 1939, he developed some of the implications of the statement by proclaiming that "personality, individuality is a biological device which has served its end in evolution and will decline." [5] By 1941, the full blossoming of the statement occurred in a thesis which he submitted for a doctorate at London University: *A Thesis on the Quality of Illusion on the Continuity of the Individual Life in the Higher Metazoa with Particular Reference to the Species Homo Sapiens.* The great advocate of the power of the individual had capitulated at last and conceded that individuality, that splendid dream of mankind, is a myth.

His capitulation, far from canceling his significance for a contemporary audience, has ironically accented it. As he was the first to introduce to the world of the novel the human implications of the rapid changes wrought by technological and scientific advancement, so, too, was he the first to introduce the problems of individuality precipitated by those changes. Like his prophecies of war and destruction, atomic bombs and tanks, his statement on individuality suggests that problem with which we must of necessity become increasingly concerned. Wells's despair reflects not so much the effects of the two world wars he could do little to avert, but that far greater problem which grows as the population multiplies and science and technology destroy more of the inherited, life-sustaining patterns and habits. His despair presents us with questions the vast dimensions of which he barely sensed in such novels as *When the Sleeper Awakes* and *The First Men in the Moon*.

Well's pronouncements of his doubts of the existence of true individuality suggest the despair of the twentieth century which has made its youth restless and which is increasingly the concern of its novelists. What he proclaims is not so much what he has concluded logically, but rather what he has developed emotionally. From the very first he declared his independence of any power outside of the human. In this declaration he shifted responsibility for the human condition from the shoulders of a deity he declared a myth, to those of the reality he saw as human progress. In this shift of responsibility, he placed too great a burden upon the individual. In his novels he became too hard a taskmaster. He would not tolerate the thousand and one frailties which cause the individual to stumble on the road to the fulfillment of his ideals, but which, nevertheless, make him human. He failed to realize in the novel as he did in reality, that to credit man with powers akin to the divine is to crush him with a responsibility his limited powers and his failings are incapable of sustaining. Though Wells affirmed it, man the individual or man collectively, as he later contended, is not God and certainly cannot be in a successful novel.

For some three decades in his works, Wells forced mankind to carry the mantle of divinity. When his faith in the species was time and time again betrayed, he retreated from his position. His final statement that man can be understood only in terms of his species and not of his individuality suggests his desire to relinquish that responsibility, which he finally realized man is incapable of fulfilling, in order to return to that safe and comfortable period in his life before he declared that "God is a lie."

6

"I Write as I Walk"
A Critical View of Wells

Like so many authors before and after him, Wells has
suffered the critical neglect which all too often follows on
the heels of wild adulation. He is not altogether without
blame for this neglect. In a period when the experimental plays so important a role in judging the quality
of a work of art, he does not nor cannot fare well. His
early prose sounds vaguely Victorian and his later bla-
tantly journalistic; and generally he writes as if Conrad,
James, and Joyce, whom he admired, had never existed.
But his neglect is not solely the result of changing
literary tastes. Wells did not help the matter any. So
much of what he wrote mitigates against an apprecia-
tion of his work in any age. There are his ideas, often
half-formed, which rush at the reader with the speed and
deadly results of a machine gun. There is his black,
doom-filled negativeness which clouds even the most
optimistic of his works. There is his insatiable and in-
sistent polemicism which crowds almost every page.
Most of all, there is the vast, bloated mass of his work
which presents a formidable barrier to the interest of
even the most avid Wellsian fan. He wrote too much and
repeated himself too often. To reverse what was said of
Dr. Johnson: had he written less and spoken more, he
would have been more successful.

To compound the matter, Wells relished the pose of

the journalist, perhaps as a defense against his critics. He enjoyed playing the part of that harassed individual —completely devoid of the taint of the artist—deeply involved in the vital affairs of the world, sleeves rolled up, busily engaged in dashing off broadsides to the public, crusading for the right and against the enemies of mankind, loudly sounding forth on the glories and the dangers of scientific discoveries and technological advances. Generations of critics, in the light of the difficulties his work presents, have taken him at his word and have dismissed him as a hack who did not pause even to revise his work.[1]

These critics are not entirely wrong. There is much in Wells that can be dismissed as journalism, but these pieces are the results of a mind vitally interested in the current affairs of his day. They also reflect an impatience and a despair on his part which grew out of the limitations he discovered in the art he practiced so diligently in the first half of his career. While he never hesitated in giving loud expression to his ideas for the salvation of mankind, he was generally reticent to discuss his art and the theory out of which it was produced. He claimed that he was not an artist. Behind his claim lies not an inability to articulate his theory of esthetics, but rather a sensitivity developed over the years. Critics had far too often and far too consistently demonstrated greater interest in his sociological ideas than the art he practiced. Fellow writers turned against him, noting that his work was a betrayal of the cause of art. Virginia Woolf was such a one. In her essay, "Mr. Bennett and Mrs. Brown," she proceeded to destroy the type of novel produced by Wells. Another was Henry James who had been his friend.[2]

No two more oddly matched individuals could be chosen for a literary relationship. The pathetic and somewhat ironic humor of their friendship is highlighted by the fact that James, an expatriate American, strove to be more English than the English whom he admired. Conrad tells the story of a visit he made to the author. Noting an odd and highly varied collection of walking sticks and headgear in James's front hall, he was about to leave believing that James was too occupied to see him. Each object, he learned after discovering that James was not entertaining visitors, was used by its owner on different but very definite occasions in imitation of what he conceived to be the English custom. Ironically, though his life was as close a copy of the English tradition as he could make it, his tightly structured novels were not. On the other hand, Wells was less than socially acceptable in his ill-fitting clothing, raffish moustache, impossible accent, and painfully squeaky voice. But he did have the reputation for writing rattling good, if rather loose and disjointed, stories which sold amazingly well. These James admired at first, despite their lack of definite structure and style contrary to the somewhat hysterical control he exercised over his own material.

James's novels never sold as well as those of the younger author. This disparity might well have been the true source of their quarrel and eventual break, and not the essentially different postures they assumed in their work. But essentially different they were. Wells, though not as genteelly English as his friend, held to the English tradition of the novel: loosely constructed, rambling, discursive, philosophical, argumentative, filled with the sights and sounds of life.[3] It was in this tradition that he produced *Tono-Bungay*, *Kipps*, *The History of Mr. Polly*, the other seriocomic novels widely accepted by a public nurtured on Dickens, and ultimately, his long polemic works. Unity, which is the product of a tight structure, might produce art, but never life. "Why should a book have unity?" Wells wrote. "For a picture it's reasonable, because you have to see it all at once. It's like wanting to have a whole country done in one style and period of architecture." [4]

Wells's insistence on the need for a free and uninhibited structure must not be understood to mean that he believed the novel should be equally free thematically. He believed, rather, that the novel has at the core of its being a vital purpose far beyond that conceived of by any of his contemporaries. The novel, he insisted, must effect "moral consequences." [5] As the population of the world grows, he insisted, and an ever-increasing multitude becomes capable of reading, some common ground must be found on which could be discussed and debated those themes of mutual importance to mankind. Out of these discussions and debates could come the answers to problems and the directions for actions which are the "moral consequences." He understood the novel to be a "social mediator, the vehicle of understanding, the instrument of self-examination, the parade of morals and the exchange of manners, the factory of customs, the criticisms of laws and institutions and of social dogmas and ideas . . . the home confessional, the initiator of knowledge, the need of self-questioning." [6]

In effect, in defining a role for the novel, Wells pleads for its relevancy in a world changing so rapidly that all of the constants, including the long-established means of communication, are losing or are in the process of losing their validity. Yet the communication of man to man, nation to nation has, paradoxically, become more important in this modern age than it has ever been in the past because misunderstanding can be the prelude to the destruction of humanity. Wells believed that any art, especially the novel because of its claim to a close relationship to life, which refuses to understand the vital role it must play in the midst of the rapid and disquieting changes of the twentieth century sows the seeds of its own destruction. No artist has the right to withdraw his work from contemporary life and expect it to live and have meaning; nor should any artist resort to the pretext that he is writing for the ages to justify such a withdrawal.

The position Wells takes is essentially the product of the two dedications of his life: science and art. Like C. P. Snow at a later date, he felt the pressing need for a close relationship of the two. As a scientist, he understood the immense value of a laboratory in providing a proving ground of theory and an arena in which man may broaden and deepen his knowledge of himself and of his world. In such antiseptic confines, the testing of theories and the exploration of the unknown can be pursued in safety and with a degree of objectivity not possible or feasible in the workaday world. Grueling and seemingly endless tests can be applied with impunity, and only when the theory has proven its stability or the unknown quantity has been completely explored and defined is the knowledge released to benefit mankind. Trial and error have their roles in the discovery of a vaccine, but these tests should not and cannot be conducted without strict control lest they prove more destructive to mankind than the evil the vaccine is intended to combat.

So too, Wells maintains, should there exist a laboratory for testing knowledge far more important to humanity than the preservation of its biological existence, important as that is. There are forces loose in the world, he realized, far more deadly than the most potent of viruses. The ends of these forces are recurring wars, social injustices, and ultimately the Armageddon he predicted. These forces are man's dark side: his disposition to violence, his hatred, his greed, his hypocrisy, his complacency. Were these moral diseases as evident in their corrosion of the human spirit as smallpox or any of the physical diseases are in their attacks on the body, man would recognize the pressing need to develop cures. It is the very inability of man to perceive the insidious workings of these black forces within himself which is their greatest strength. All the more reason, Wells affirmed, for exposing and destroying them in a laboratory where all their deviousness can be revealed. Wells understood the novel as such a laboratory. Within its antiseptic confines man's spiritual illnesses can be dissected and examined; battles can be fought without the spilling of blood; ideas and ideals can be argued and tested without the destruction of their creators; modes of conduct can be explored without harm to the principals; direction can be offered to the confused; insight can be given to the bewildered. In short, the novelist may once again assume the roles of prophet and teacher which the creative artist has long played, and out of whose hands they were torn only in the recent past. The novelist can forecast the future, warn his readers against its dangers, and urge them with all the passion at his command to take the proper course of action, the proper paths which will lead humanity from certain doom to that millennia for which it longs.

Wells attempted to perform such tasks in his own work. In some instances, his predictions have proven uncannily true. He foresaw the atomic bomb and the physical, spiritual, and emotional horrors it has visited and will visit upon mankind. He forecast a growing technology and a population explosion which would result in much the same difficulties we are presently encountering in our urban areas.[7] What he attempted to do in his own work, he believed, was not duplicated in the work of his contemporaries. For him, James represented a prime example of that isolation produced, ironically, by the artist himself who insists upon relinquishing his vital, contemporary role and withdrawing within the walls of his art by ignoring the swift changes taking place in the real world about him. Wells saw no point in involving oneself in the eternal verities if, in doing so, one overlooks the present, more pressing truths. He was aware that his insistence upon topicality in the novel was condemning much of his work to oblivion. Nevertheless, he continued to demand that the novel must give meaning and direction to the present, even if its value for the future is destroyed in the process.

Paradoxically, despite his insistence upon timeliness, he did produce works which have endured and have held the public's interest long after their first success. None of these, however, live because they carry Wells's messages to the world. They live because they manage to capture and hold attention through their essentially honest statements about the human condition. Among these more lasting works are his science fiction novels which have been often copied but never surpassed. They have set the pattern for countless monsters from Mars, visits to the outer reaches of space and time, and experiments which convey man to new and strange dimensions of his being. They have also set the pattern for the themes which control contemporary science fiction as well as suggest those which permeate almost every form of the contemporary novel. There are those themes which treat of man in search of his identity in a world increasingly dedicated to the mass rather than the individual; man versus the terrible consequences of progress, be it technological or scientific; man and his attempt to control his destiny through a development of his own potentialities. But it is not Wells's science fiction alone which has survived. There are his seriocomic novels, one of which, *Tono-Bungay*, has found its way into the standard college course in the modern British novel. Here, too, Wells touches a theme familiar to the reader of the twentieth-century novel—the individual struggling to establish his identity in a world more comfortable for the conformist rather than the rebel.

Because Wells saw little of the relevancy he hoped to give his own work in the novels of his contemporaries, he dealt rather harshly with his fellow writers. He spoke of them as seekers after lasting fame rather than present effectiveness. Again, there is a suggestion in his vehemence of one who is aware that he is incapable of achieving such fame. But there is no point here in pursuing the reasons for the position he took. Suffice it to say that Wells's beliefs shaped and directed the manner in which he wrote, and ultimately these beliefs drove him out of the confines of the novel into less disguised polemicism.

It is important to note, however, that much of his plea for the relevancy of the novel, while he was still producing such work, devolves upon the direction he believed must be given the form if it is to result in the required "moral consequences" of which he speaks. He held that this direction must be completely personal and not objective as James insisted in their correspondence. In involving himself personally, the author becomes one with the reader and the two jointly explore the problem at hand.

Wells suggests further that the author has no emotional or logical right to objectivity. Certainly he has no moral right. For Wells, the author's personal involvement in his novel is a moral obligation. Once he identifies within the events of his own life the sources of the social, moral, or political problems he is to treat, he must realize that they also exist in his readers. As a member of humanity, he cannot divorce himself from the matter discussed in the novel because he is involved by his very nature. In the same way, he cannot divorce himself logically because of the nature of creativity. Wells held, somewhat scientifically, that nothing can be "created" in the strictest sense of the word. Every character, every event, every theme, is fundamentally a "compilation" a "fabrication" frankly or furtively drawn from life.[8] Creativity is essentially a synthesizing process. To attempt to divorce oneself entirely from the process is as illogical as it is impossible. Even if a remote possibility of such a separation existed, it would not be wise for the author to attempt to achieve it. To succeed would spell certain death for the work. Wells insisted that only by giving of himself—and by this he means the very facts of his life, his thoughts, his opinions—consciously or unconsciously, does the writer breathe the spirit of life into his work.[9]

But Wells does not leave the argument at this point. True, the vital force the author imparts to his work flows from a personal involvement and an intimate relationship with it established out of the fabric of his own life. Another element, nevertheless, is necessary. Logically, if the characters, episodes, themes are drawn from life, they must be fixed in structures which resemble life as closely as it is possible for the written word to do so. To do otherwise is not to confer life on the work, but death. Life is loose, formless, unpatterned, filled with irrelevancies, discursive, lacking completeness. So too, Wells insisted, should be the structure of the novel.[10] If the novel is to effect the all-important "moral consequences" the novelist must convince the reader that what he is reading is true.[11] Balance, unity, finish mitigate against the "trueness" of a work because it is manifest even to the most unsophisticated reader that life is in no way so neat.

Wells held that what is true of character, episode, theme, and structure also must be true of the language employed in the novel. It too must be identified with life. He was not, however, always successful in reaching this ideal in his own work, much of which suffers from the stiffness and awkwardness inherited from the Victorian period. Nevertheless, he makes a valiant attempt. His belief suggests an awareness on his part of the large and important role language was to play in the twentieth-century novel. He strove for the uncomplicated sentence, a simple and "instinctive" vocabulary—the happy word rather than a bookish and labored substitute. All this reminds one of the later accomplishments of Hemingway and others who strove to capture the cadences of speech on the written page. Out of discussions with James, Conrad, and later Ford Maddox Hueffer (Ford) came a crystallization of Wells's style. "I write as I walk because I want to get somewhere and I write as straight as I can, because that is the best way to get there." [12]

Obviously, Wells believed that the "there" and the "somewhere" are far more important than the route taken—the importance of the "moral consequences" outweighs the style employed. This theory spelled honesty for Wells. His judgments of others accents what he thought of any other theory of style. Other writers—he did not name them, but meant most certainly James and Conrad—"dress their souls before the glass, add a few final touches of makeup and sally forth like old bucks for fresh 'adventures among masterpieces.' I come upon masterpieces by pure chance; they happen to me and I do not worry about what I miss." [13]

The durability of his work seemingly never entered his mind. Preoccupation with the reception of one's novels in the future results in their death for the present because the artist must, to insure their survival, divorce them from the present and, more significantly, from the vast majority of contemporary readers. They must be written for the cognoscenti who are able to perceive that they have value for the ages rather than for the contemporary world. This knowledgeable few can nurture them and pass them on to that age which can more fully appreciate them. Essentially, the novels which endure beyond their own time must be chiefly experimental. Wells's comments on Joyce's *Work in Progress* point out the results of such experimentation. He saw in Joyce's manipulation of language an "extraordinary experiment," but ultimately a "dead end." [14] Joyce, in his estimation, had pushed the novel to the brink of its own destruction as a form by denying, through the language barriers he had erected, whatever opportunities it had for effecting the "moral consequences" Wells held so dear. Joyce had become misdirected in his mission as an artist. By denying intelligibility to so many, he had surrendered his vital role as prophet and teacher and retreated from an age which pleads for direction, understanding, help.

Ironically, it was his heeding this very call for direction, understanding, and help which ultimately led Wells out of the realm of the novel. As he became increasingly involved and concerned with the problems of a world moving relentlessly toward a second global confrontation, he became more vividly aware of the limitations of the form in terms of its ability to effect real and lasting changes in mankind's warlike posture. With the appearance of *The World of William Clissold* (1926), he all but abandoned the writing of novels. A talky, two-volume, plotless compendium of Wellsian ideas and ideals, the book pointed the direction the remainder of his writing would take, except for brief lapses into the old Wellsian world of the imagination.

The *Outline of History* and similar outpourings from his pen failed to endear him to the intellectuals of the 1930s, who found his warnings of future doom and prescriptions for peace dull and unconvincing. Ironically, these direct statements of his beliefs were less influential than his earlier flights of imagination which caught and held the minds of two generations. There was no writer who emerged in the thirties who could state, as Kenneth

Rexroth did in his autobiography, that Wells's work of that period directly shaped his thinking.[15] This is not the phase of Wells's work which will be remembered. Nor, as some current critics maintain, will much else survive.[16] This is not the point. What cannot be denied Wells is his proper place in the development of literature in this twentieth century.

Wells came at a stifling period in England's history when an age, the Victorian, had long outlived those vital forces which moved men to think and act for the good of their species. He came at a period which was growing more and more content with the lifeless formulas of society and growing more and more impervious to needed changes in those formulas. He came at a period when the masses were growing more and more conscious of the power which was in their numbers. He came when a new age, the Edwardian, and a new century, the twentieth, were waiting expectantly to take their places at the center of the stage. He came when science and technology were beginning to make the first great advances into the ignorance which had clouded humanity for so many centuries. He came when these advances were effecting rapid changes in all aspects of man's life save one, seemingly, the novel. Paradoxically, these effects which were altering life so radically were ignored by an art which prided itself on its close relationship to that life. Wells was one of the first to sense the great need to probe in the realm of the novel the growing social and moral unrest occasioned by the applications of the discoveries of this new science and technology to the long unchanged conditions of man's daily life. In doing so he discovered and discussed many of the major social, psychological, and moral questions which plague us today and are as yet unanswered satisfactorily.

His greatest fault, however, was his fundamental inability to develop his suspicions that these problems are not solely the province of contemporary man, nor solely attributable to scientific and technological advances, nor to a deadening social system, but have plagued man throughout his existence. He failed to understand that these problems rise up out of man's nature. In his failure to come directly to grip with the root cause of humanity's difficulties, he supplied answers that were and are too simple to believe and too idealistic to be completely achieved. As a result, he committed the unpardonable aesthetic sin of misreading human nature and translating this misreading into characters who became merely puppets for their creator to move as he willed. He reduced human nature to rigid, immutable, and predictable patterns. He divided humanity into two camps: the good who espoused Wellsian philosophy without argument, and the evil who rejected it and as a consequence were condemned. Eventually, he failed to see any good in those he considered evil nor any evil in those whom he considered good. But he did all of this for a reason—his love of mankind and his fear for its future. In loving mankind so much, he lost, ironically, a love for man. Like Swift, whom he somewhat resembles, he failed to discern the glory of man which lies behind man's stupidities, his inconsistencies, cantankerousness, and the evil he does. Consequently, Wells failed in the first immutable requirement of the novel—that its creator love his creatures. Wells paid the full price for his failure—despair in his later years and oblivion for much of his work.

Notes

Introduction

1. *New York Times*, 19 May 1969, pp. 1, 56.
2. The annotated bibliography of Wells which I produce periodically for *English Literature in Transition* has shown since its inception a marked increase in the number of items listed.
3. Others include Harris Wilson's editon of the Bennett-Wells correspondence (London, 1960) and R. A. Gettmann's similar service for the Gissing-Wells correspondence (London, 1962). Both volumes owe their existence, as does so much of recent Wells scholarship, to the repository of Wells's papers at the Urbana campus of the University of Illinois.

1 – The End of the World: Youth and The Time Machine

1. *First and Last Things* (New York, 1918), p. 128.
2. No definitive bibliography of Wells's work exists nor is there any indication that one will be forthcoming in the near future despite the efforts of the Wells Society which has produced what they call *A Comprehensive Bibliography* (London, 1966). Its introduction claims that in no way is it definitive.
3. *Experiment in Autobiography* (New York, 1934), p. 45.
4. For a graphic picture of life on a bare subsistence level

at this time see the early chapters of Charles Chaplin's *My Autobiography* (New York, 1964).

5. *First and Last Things*, p. 131.

6. *God the Invisible King* (New York, 1917), p. 376.

7. Ibid., p. 138.

8. Ibid., p. 389.

9. Ibid., p. 391.

2 – The Search for Salvation Begins

1. *God the Invisible King* (New York, 1917), pp. 490–91.

2. *First and Last Things* (New York, 1918), p. 128.

3. *Experiment in Autobiography* (New York, 1934), p. 122; the principle is somewhat enlarged and dramatized in its appearance at the beginning of chapter 9 of *The History of Mr. Polly* (New York, 1951).

4. *History of Mr. Polly*, p. 232.

5. Ibid., p. 262.

6. Ibid., p. 293.

7. *First and Last Things*, pp. 150–51, 290.

8. Ibid., p. 150.

9. *Athenaeum*, October 1918, p. 437; *Spectator* (London), 16 November 1918; *Saturday Review* (London), 5 October 1918, p. 917.

10. *Experiment in Autobiography*, p. 420.

11. *First and Last Things*, pp. 150–51.

12. Ibid., p. 287.

13. Ibid., p. 290.

14. *A Variety of Men* (New York, 1968).

15. *First and Last Things*, pp. 272–73.

3 – Inferno

1. Bernard Bergonzi also records in his *The Early H. G. Wells* (Manchester, 1961) some of the furor which sur-

rounded its publication. He notes, interestingly, that "there was a tendency to attack the book as though it were sexually offensive, even though this was not the case" (pp. 97–99).

2. *Saturday Review* (London), 21 December 1895, p. 843.

3. *Spectator* (London), 19 June 1897, p. 871.

4. Ingvold Raknem, *H. G. Wells and His Critics.* (Trondheim, Norway, 1962), pp. 337–39.

4 – Paradiso: The World State

1. *God the Invisible King* (New York, 1917), pp. 458–59.

2. *The World Set Free* (New York, 1914), p. 242.

3. *The Outline of History* (London, 1961), pp. 1195–96.

5 – Apocalypse

1. Richard Hauer Costa, *H. G. Wells* (New York, 1967), p. 145.

2. *Mind at the End of its Tether* (New York, 1945), p. 17.

3. Ibid., p. 17.

4. *First and Last Things* (London, 1908), pp. 92–93.

5. *Points of View* (London, 1939), p. 66.

6 – "I Write as I Walk": A Critical View of Wells

1. This charge is not entirely valid. Frank Swinnerton, a friend of Wells, reports in his *Background with Chorus* (London, 1956) that he observed numerous revisions by Wells of his works which extended to the galley sheets.

2. Not all of the literary luminaries of his day were against him. E. M. Forster (*Art of the Novel*, New York, 1927) was a notable exception. Forster championed the

Wellsian method and was one of the first to note Wells's debt to Dickens and the English tradition of the novel.

3. "The Contemporary Novel," in *Henry James to H. G. Wells* (Urbana, Ill., 1958), p. 138.

4. *Boon* (London, 1915), p. 103.

5. *The Work of H. G. Wells* (London, 1927) 1, xiii.

6. "The Contemporary Novel," p. 150.

7. W. Warren Wagar's excellent compilation, *H. G. Wells: Journalism and Prophecy 1893–1946* (New York, 1964), records many of the difficulties Wells predicted.

8. *Experiment in Autobiography*, p. 306.

9. *The Work of H. G. Wells*, 14, x.

10. "The Contemporary Novel," pp. 136, 140.

11. Ibid., p. 143.

12. *Experiment in Autobiography*, p. 532.

13. Ibid., p. 532.

14. Giselle Freund and V. B. Carleton, *James Joyce in Paris: His Final Years* (New York, 1965), p. 90.

15. Kenneth Rexroth, *An Autobiographical Novel* (Garden City, N.Y., 1966), p. 95. Rexroth has high praise for Wells's work in general. Most specifically, however, he cites *The Research Magnificent* as the volume which "has influenced my life more than any other."

16. Bernard Bergonzi maintains that only Well's imaginative works created in the early part of his career have any literary value and that it is "axiomatic that the bulk of Wells's published output has lost whatever *literary* interest it might have and is not likely to regain it in the foreseeable future." *The Early H. G. Wells* (Manchester, 1961), p. 165.

Selected Bibliography

Primary Sources

The following bibliography lists only those works cited in the text. It is pointless, and indeed impossible, to list all of Wells's published material since much is out of print and difficult to come by. Most of the titles listed, however, are readily available, especially his science fiction which has appeared countless times and in many cheap editions. There have also been many collections of Wells's work but by far the most important is the Atlantic Edition (New York, 1924–27). Its chief claim to fame are the prefaces Wells wrote for each volume, wherein he outlined his purpose and discussed his method.

It is difficult to imagine that there exists anyone who has not read or encountered through the motion pictures, television, or the theatre at least one of Wells's novels, so continuously popular have they been with the public. If such a person does exist, he would do best were he to select as his introduction *Seven Science Fiction Novels of H. G. Wells* (New York, 1950). This collection contains the best tales he has written including *The Time Machine, War of the Worlds,* and *The Invisible Man. Tono-Bungay* and *The History of Mr. Polly* are excellent representatives of his realistic fiction. Those who have seen the stage musical and motion picture, *Half a Sixpence,* might enjoy reading *Kipps,* from which they were made. As a sample of his nonfiction, *The Outline of History* should be read provided that one understands he is not reading history recorded objectively.

Anatomy of Frustration. London, 1936.

Ann Veronica. London, 1909.

The Autocracy of Mr. Parnham. London, 1930.

Babes in the Darkling Wood. London, 1940.

Boon. London, 1931.

British Nationalism and the League of Nations. London, 1919.

Complete Short Stories. London, 1966.

The Dream. London, 1924.

Elements of Reconstruction. London, 1916.

First and Last Things. London, 1908.

The First Men in the Moon, in *Seven Science Fiction Novels of H. G. Wells.* New York, 1950.

The Food of the Gods, in *Seven Science Fiction Novels of H. G. Wells.* New York, 1950.

A Forecast of the World's Affairs. London, 1928.

God the Invisible King. London, 1917.

The History of Mr. Polly. New York, 1951.

The Holy Terror. London, 1939.

Idea of a League of Nations. London, 1918.

In the Days of the Comet, in *Seven Science Fiction Novels of H. G. Wells.* New York, 1950.

In the Fourth Year. London, 1918.

The Invisible Man, in *Seven Science Fiction Novels of H. G. Wells.* New York, 1950.

The Island of Dr. Moreau, in *Seven Science Fiction Novels of H. G. Wells.* New York, 1950.

Joan and Peter. New York, 1917.

Kipps: The Story of a Simple Soul. London, 1905.

Love and Mr. Lewisham. London, 1900.

Men Like Gods. London, 1923.

Mind at the End of Its Tether. New York, 1945.

Modern Utopia. London, 1909.

Mr. Blettsworthy on Rampole Island. London, 1928.

Mr. Britling Sees It Through. London, 1915.

The New Machiavelli. London, 1911.

The Outline of History. London, 1961.

The Passionate Friends. New York, 1913.

The Plattner Story and Others. London, 1897.

Playing at Peace. London, 1927.

Points of View. London, 1939.

The Research Magnificent. London, 1915.

Salvaging of Civilization. London, 1921.

The Shape of Things to Come. London, 1933.

The Soul of a Bishop. London, 1917.

Tales of Space and Time. London, 1899.

A Thesis on the Quality of Illusion in the Continuity of the Individual Life in the Higher Metazoa, with Particular Reference to the Species Homo Sapiens. London, 1941.

The Time Machine, in *Seven Science Fiction Novels of H. G. Wells*. New York, 1950.

Tono-Bungay. New York, 1935.

Twelve Stories and a Dream. London, 1903.

The War in the Air. London, 1908.

The War of the Worlds, in *Seven Science Fiction Novels of H. G. Wells*. New York, 1950.

The War That Will End War. London, 1914.

The Way to a League of Nations. London, 1919.

The Wheels of Chance. London, 1896.

When the Sleeper Awakes. London, 1899.

The Wife of Sir Isaac Harman. London, 1914.

The Wonderful Visit. London, 1926.

The World Set Free. London, 1914.

You Can't Be Too Careful. London, 1941.

Secondary Sources

Few writers have drawn forth so great a volume of commentary while still living as has H. G. Wells. Too much, however, treats of the obvious, and more is repetitive. Still more is petulant in the manner in which it defends those sacred cows Wells loved to attack. Most is useless as an aid to understanding so cantankerous an individual. This list represents an attempt to cull these items to produce a bibliography which should contribute to a general knowledge of Wells and his work. Notably lacking is a definitive biography which has not and should not see the light of day for some time to come, since so many individuals who were emotionaly involved with Wells are still alive. Nor is any definitive bibliography listed. None exists and there is little likelihood that one will be produced. Wells simply wrote too much. He often changed publishers and tossed off bits of journalism whenever a cause warranted comment.

Belgion, Montgomery. *H. G. Wells*. London, 1953.

Bergonzi, Bernard. *The Early H. G. Wells*. Manchester, 1961.

Borrello, Alfred. "Annotated Bibliography of H. G. Wells," *English Literature in Transition*, beginning in the Fall 1968 issue.

Braybrooke, Patrick. *Some Aspects of H. G. Wells*. London, 1928.

Brome, Vincent. *H. G. Wells*. London, 1951.

Brooks, Van Wyck. *The World of H. G. Wells*. New York, 1915.

Chappell, Fred A. *Bibliography of H. G. Wells*. London, 1928.

Connes, George A. A *Dictionary of the Characters and Scenes in the Novels, Romances and Short Stories of H. G. Wells*. Dijon, France, 1926.

Costa, Richard Hauer. *H. G. Wells*. New York, 1967.

Dark, Sidney. *An Outline of H. G. Wells, the Superman in the Street*. New York, 1922.

Dickson, Lovat. *H. G. Wells: His Turbulent Life and Times*. New York, 1969.

Edel, Leon and Gordon Ray, eds. *Henry James to H. G. Wells*. Urbana, Illinois, 1958.

Forest, D. W. "The Modern Religion of H. G. Wells," *Expositor*, 14 (1917), 437–46.

Forster, Edward Morgan. *Aspects of the Novel*. New York, 1954.

Freund, Giselle and V. B. Carleton. *James Joyce in Paris: His Final Years*. New York, 1965.

Raknem, Ingvold. *H. G. Wells and His Critics.* Trondheim, Norway, 1962.

Rexroth, Kenneth. *An Autobiographical Novel.* Garden City, N.Y., 1966.

Snow, Charles Percy. A *Variety of Men.* New York, 1968.

Swinnerton, Frank. *Background with Chorus.* London, 1956.

Wagar, W. Warren. *H. G. Wells and the World State.* New Haven, 1961.

―――. *H. G. Wells, Journalism and Prophecy 1893–1946.* Boston, 1965.

Weeks, Robert. *H. G. Wells as a Sociological Novelist.* Ann Arbor, Michigan, 1952.

Wells, Geoffrey. *The Works of H. G. Wells 1897–1925, a Bibliography, Dictionary and Subject Index.* London, 1926.

The H. G. Wells Society. *H. G. Wells: A Comprehensive Bibliography.* London, 1966.

Wilson, Harris, ed. *Arnold Bennett and H. G. Wells. A Record of a Personal and Literary Friendship.* London, 1960.

Index